Designing and making stage scenery

Designing and making stage scenery

Michael Warre

Foreword by Peter Brook

Studio Vista London
Reinhold Book Corporation
New York

For J.L.

The author wishes to thank the artists who
have kindly allowed their designs to be
reproduced in this book.

© Michael Warre 1966
Reprinted 1968
First Published in Great Britain by Studio Vista Limited
Blue Star House, Highgate Hill, London N19
And in the United States by Reinhold Book Corporation
430 Park Avenue, New York, New York 10022
Library of Congress Catalog Card Number: 66-23646
Distributed in Canada by General Publishing Co. Ltd
30 Lesmill Road, Don Mills, Ontario
Set in 11 on 12-pt. Plantin
Illustrations printed by Higginson and Harris Ltd
Text printed in Great Britain by Staples Printers Limited

SBN 289 36885 5

Contents

List of plates

Foreword

Years ago I went on a pilgrimage to Gordon Craig. This was the man who had brought simplicity into our theatre; the man who had swept away the clutter and rubbish of Victorian scenery, the visionary who saw the stage as a temple, lofty and pure. We spoke about such serious themes, then he began to reminisce, about his own youthful idol, Henry Irving. His eyes sparkled as he conjured up the red curtain, the painted forest, the surprise vista, the false perspective, the cunning *trompes l'œil*, the magic of that theatre he had so successfully destroyed. Seventy years later, he still savoured it with joy.

I understood this love-hate. I share it. Scenery is irresistibly fascinating. For me, the theatre always begins with an image. If I find the image through the design, I know how to continue with the production. If I go into rehearsal with a nagging sense that the set is not right, I know I will never find my way out again. My most cherished theatre-going memories are of Bérard; Bérard the man, the gentle, bearded genius, always searching, always starting anew – and Bérard, the designer, the greatest of stage magicians, with his tiny sliding white porticos in Amphitryon, his shimmering blue skeleton of a café in La Folle de Chaillot, his haunting and austere formality of greys in Don Juan. In human terms, my closest relationships have been with designers. Nothing makes me happier than to take a piece of cardboard and begin to fold and tear it into a set myself.

Yet over the years I have worked always against scenery – in reaction away from scenery. When Rolf Gerard and I did *Romeo and Juliet* at Stratford we began throwing out our own scenery at the dress rehearsal. Gradually we came down to an empty orange arena, a few sticks – and the wings were full of elaborate and expensive discarded units. We were very proud of ourselves, but the management was furious and we weren't invited back for many years.

Nothing is so beautiful as a bare stage: yet its loneliness and its openness is often too strong a statement and it must be enclosed. How? What objects should be put into this great void? The problem is always agonising. Not too little. Not too much. What is appropriate?

At first I used to think of the stage as a world; I used to believe that our task was to create a place in which the action could naturally unfold. After all, a play is about life and life is a relation between people and the world that surrounds them. But the stage picture made not one world, but two – one for the actors, another for the audience.

Then it seemed that our task was to provide a machine, a special machine for each play, in which the requirements for each moment appear when wanted, then vanish again.

Now, I believe that as in a film the image of a play is continuous and cumulative. The set by itself and the costume by itself have no meaning, no value – one has too often been disappointed by the costume, beautiful at dress parades, that loses its beauty when seen in the sweep of the action – like the beautiful rushes in the cinema, which look far less splendid when placed in the context of the story. I believe today that design means creating possibilities for a continually moving and evolving set of images that need have no consistency, no stability, no architecture, but which spin out of the actors' themes and play on the audience just at the moment when they unfold. They should parallel the rich and formless impressions of the world we live in. Yet behind this is the call to classicism, the constant wish to give form, to impose order again. But what form? Whose order?

Michael Warre has worked in and understands every known form of theatre. He has designed at L.A.M.D.A. the perfect instrument for experiment. In his book, with clarity and skill, he traces the glittering and romantic traditions that have made stages full and empty in turn. In his last paragraph he presents the question so well that his words should be hung up at every stage door for actors, directors and authors as well as designers to observe: SELECTION OF THE SIGNIFICANT DETAIL – REJECTION OF THE UNIMPORTANT COMMENT. It's not as easy as it sounds.

PETER BROOK

Preface

The nineteen-sixties will be seen by posterity to have been a great period of rebirth in the theatre. New playhouses are springing up all over Europe and America. Playwrights are voicing new ideas and airing subjects considered taboo for generations past. Architects are planning new buildings, unconventional in concept. Stage designers are handling new materials which are lighter, more tensile and flexible than ever known before. There is a great swing away from the old gilt and plush theatres that we have known for so long.

These old playhouses developed slowly through the years, from the candle-lit halls of medieval castles into the court theatres of the seventeenth century, with formal scenery on raked platforms lit by oil lamps and chandeliers. In the eighteenth century, theatres all over Europe became larger, requiring a more complex arrangement of seating in tiers, bigger stages and more scenery. The introduction of gas lighting, and the dousing of the candelabra in the auditorium, finally pushed the actor behind a frame, from which he was only to be released by the unlimited flexibility of electric light.

Throughout history the lighting of the stage has swayed the designer between two fundamental approaches to making scenery – flat or solid, illusion or reality. The open air demands solid architecture, gas lighting requires flat painted scenery. Fashion, too, has swung between the formal and the natural, but it will be seen that the greatest designers have usually combined both approaches.

After two hundred years of flat scenery, it was the advent of electric light that enabled designers with the vision of Gordon Craig and Adolphe Appia to realize that the play of light upon surfaces and textures can create an atmosphere more powerfully than gallons of paint.

We are the inheritors of centuries of experiment in the theatre. It is impossible to write about scenic design without tracing its history first. That is why this book is divided into two parts: the first historical, the second practical. For we must go back to the origins of drama, and see the different ways of staging plays in other times and civilizations. Only then can we begin to know how to use this marvellous place – the stage – on which anything can be made to happen.

1 Background

The origins of theatre lie hidden beyond the distance of recorded history. We can only guess at the rituals of human sacrifice, the invocations of rain, the fertility rites and the harvest celebrations that were modified into the first forms of drama. Echoes of many primitive festivals are present in our calendar, and open or hidden allusions are present in all drama. The theatre still contains a sense of awe, of wonder, release and fulfilment. The play is as old as the myth – as old as religion. It is therapeutic, dispels fear, demands participation and provides atonement. From Aeschylus to Albee the function of drama has remained the same, although the scenic background has changed from civilization to civilization – sometimes from generation to generation. The scenic designer today has centuries of theatrical experience upon which to draw, and his scenery is bound to reflect or to comment on the styles of the past. In designing scenery the knowledge of past successes and failures is naturally invaluable, and this knowledge is intimately concerned with the way that the architectural form of the theatre has developed through the centuries.

The earliest form of staging grew out of religious myth and ritual. This is true not only of ancient Greece, India, China and Japan, but also of the middle ages in Europe. To begin with there was no contrived setting – symbolic costume was more important than scenic background. This emphasis can still be seen in the classical Chinese theatre and in the Japanese No-Play. The importance of costume and the significance of furniture and properties as opposed to scenery has become a dominant factor in modern Open Stage and Arena production. For the designer there is just as much hard thinking about what to leave out as there is about what to put in. An implication can be more forceful than a statement.

GREECE

The first recorded world première was a dramatic contest in Athens, won by Thespis in 535 BC. The significance of this particular contest was that hitherto a whole drama had been performed only by a chorus, singing, intoning and dancing a story in honour of the god Dionysos. Thespis introduced an actor – presumably himself – who conducted a conversation with the chorus leader. The actor became known as the Protagonist; and this was the beginning of drama as we know it. Dialogue added another dimension. None of the words of Thespis have survived, and we have to jump sixty years for the earliest known Greek tragedy.

As far as we know, the first organized theatre was that of Dionysos Eleuthereos at Athens. Contests were held every year, in which three authors each brought out four plays – three tragedies followed by a burlesque called a Satyr play. The chorus performed on a circular dancing place called the Orkestra, which was about 78 ft in diameter. In the centre of the orkestra was the sacrificial table and altar, the Thymele. The spectators sat on the natural bowl-shaped hill more than half surrounding the orkestra. This came to be known as the Theatron – the seeing place – which is the origin of our word 'theatre'.

From the internal evidence of the plays, existing records of the festivals and from architectural remains, scholars and archaeologists have conjectured (not always in

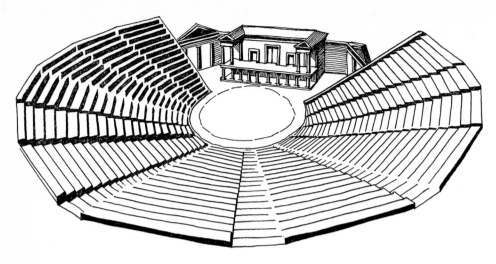

FIG 1   Bird's eye view of a Greek theatre

concord) how the plays were presented. As the drama had grown out of choral dancing, the orkestra was naturally the centre of the action. The first protagonist could have stood on the steps of the thymele to address the chorus; but as the telling of the story became more dramatic, the protagonist was required to play more than one character. This meant that he had to change his costume and mask. Even before the introduction of further actors a dressing room had become necessary. The obvious place for this was on the far side of the orkestra; so they put up a Skene – which simply means a tent – in which the actors could change their costumes and masks during the course of the choral interludes, and reappear as new characters. The front of the skene was later to become decorated, and from it our word scene is derived.

The popular Spanish, Flemish and English theatres of the sixteenth century all followed the logical pattern of placing the actors' dressing room at the back of a scaffold stage, hidden from the audience by curtains or doors. Almost any play written in Europe before the middle of the seventeenth century can be presented on a scaffold with three entrances and sometimes a window or gallery above. This form of booth theatre erected in a market square, fairground or dry river bed is common to all civilizations. Most of the audience stand and look up at the stage, unless they have more fortunate access to a courtyard window or specially built seating. The other basic form of theatre – represented nowadays by the open stage – is virtually a return to the Greek orkestra, scaled down and put indoors. It has been demonstrated that even plays written in a naturalistic convention, like Chechov's *Uncle Vanya*, can gain in impact when played upon an open stage. This is because the most direct contact between actor and audience occurs when the stage is partly enfolded by spectators – and not when the actor is seen through a frame. Open stage productions do not hamper the designer's art – they give it another dimension.

The Greeks built a wide narrow platform in front of the skene, which they called the Proskenion. Sophocles had reduced the chorus size and increased the number of speaking actors to three. These three actors, with changes of mask and costume, were capable of acting all the parts in a tragedy. Euripides added silent parts – children, nurses and servants – who also emerged from the skene on to the proskenion to play their parts. It is easy to see how the word, changed by the Romans into proscenium, has come to mean the stage frame, and still retain its original meaning – in front of scene.

During the great period of Greek drama the skene and proskenion were certainly temporary structures of wood, socketed each year into stone foundations. This suggests that the design of the stage need not always have been the same, and that the placing of the doors and the painting of the wall of the skene may have varied from year to year. This is only conjecture. What follows is a description of the later Greek theatres based on surviving stone remains.

At Athens the height of the stage or proskenion is calculated to have been about 13 ft above the orkestra. Among six other theatres of slightly later date 10 ft was the average. This height above the chorus, coupled with the fact that the actor wore a raised boot (Kothornos) and an over life-sized mask, gave a curiously magical and awesome appearance to the protagonist and his two assistants. The chorus wore no masks. They entered the orkestra from the Parodos each side and performed only in the orkestra. On each side of the proskenion wings were built out towards the theatron. They were called the Paraskenia and had a special significance: a character entering from stage left was from the city; from stage right he was assumed to have come from the harbour or from distant lands.

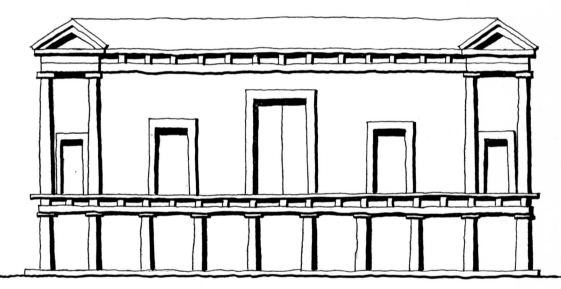

FIG 2   Conjectural drawing of a wooden skene towards the end of the fifth century BC. Flying machinery could have been housed in the gables of the Pareskenia each side

The historian Pollux, writing in the second century AD, tells us of some of the machinery used in the Greek theatres. He mentions trap-doors, hoists, cranes, lightning and thunder machines, devices for revealing dead bodies – rolled or swung out on what today we would call 'trucks' or 'waggons'. He also describes the Periaktoi which were revolving prisms painted differently on each facet, and the Mechane for lowering a god at the appropriate moment. Whether all these devices were used by the Greeks in the fifth century BC is doubtful, though we do know that dead bodies had to be revealed mechanically as slaughter was not allowed to be enacted on the stage; and we know that Euripides lowered the occasional god from above to round off the action of the play.

The Roman theatre had no profound religious significance. It was purely a place of entertainment, used not only for plays adapted from the Greek but also for gladiatorial displays and contests. To start with only temporary wooden structures were allowed – for a Roman holiday. The first permanent theatre was built by Pompey in 55 BC. It is said to have seated 10,000 spectators, and that at its inauguration 500 lions and 20 elephants were disposed of by gladiators. One of Rome's most impressive ruins today is the theatre of Marcellus which was completed about 13 BC. All over the Empire theatres sprang up, from Africa and Asia Minor across France to England, where the foundations at St Albans can be seen today.

The difference between a Greek and a Roman theatre is immediately apparent. The Greeks always chose a natural slope of the ground for the spectators to look down on the orkestra. The Romans nearly always constructed a whole building on

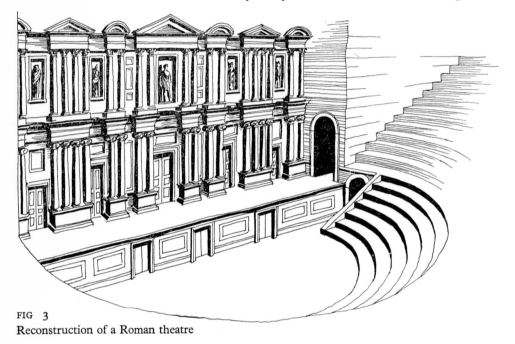

FIG 3
Reconstruction of a Roman theatre

a flat site, with passages and entrances below the Cavea where the audience sat. They also sliced the orkestra in half, making an exact semicircle and joining the sides of the stage to the sides of the cavea. The chorus disappeared and with it the parados: the spectators, wild beasts and gladiators entered and left by various Vomitoria which debouched under the cavea.

From this it will be seen that the Roman theatre became a unified building containing both audience and actor. The half orchestra (Roman spelling now) was used for combats and displays, when not filled with seats. The designer – in this case the architect – built an elaborate permanent setting of pillars and pillasters framing the three doors on the back wall – the Frons Scaenae. The stage was wide and shallow and the playing on it must have been rather like a front cloth act. In fact to reproduce the conditions of the performance of a farce by Plautus or a comedy by Terence in the second and third centuries BC, the modern designer would only have to build an architectural façade pierced by three doors, and set across the stage about 10 ft up from the footlights. The doors would have to be built solidly, because a great deal of battering and bolting goes on in these plays.

Frequently an actor says, 'Hark I hear the door creak!' – anticipating the entrance of another. The doors in the frons scaenae represented three houses. The stage was always a street, and there were also two side openings for street entrances. A character could exit left and return right by means of an imaginary street running behind the three houses. Later on the doors were increased to five, and there is evidence in some theatres of holes in the masonry where beams could have supported a roof over the stage.

We know little of the theatre in early Christian Europe. By the sixth century all organized dramatic spectacles had been stopped, and in the east the Saracen invasions destroyed most of the Imperial theatres. Nothing is known of the continuity of theatre craft, save passing references to mimes, acrobats and minstrels who wandered through Europe in the dark ages.

FIG   4   Diagram of the acting area in a Roman theatre, showing the lower story of the frons scaenae with wide, shallow stage in front

INDIA

While Catholic Europe was slowly absorbing pagan customs and, unknown to itself, preparing to re-fertilize the ancient art of the theatre, Sanskrit drama was flourishing in India. We do not know its origins or the date of its earliest compositions; nor do we know exactly in what way these charming plays were presented, as the tradition faded out in the fourteenth century. We can only guess from the plays that the stage management was very simple, but the acting and movement most sophisticated.

The *Natya Sastra* by Bharata is a treatise on the Sanskrit theatre. It existed in the second century AD, and records a tradition that may well go back to 100 BC. The treatise is extremely thorough and covers all aspects of production. A whole chapter is devoted to theatre architecture, in which Bharata describes the rectangular, square and triangular theatres and their proportions, the proper days on which to lay the foundations and the correct symbolic colours for the main posts and beams to be painted so as to encourage good spirits and to keep away malevolent ones. A few years ago the foundations of a third century playhouse were unearthed at Nagarjunakonda showing a large auditorium, square stage and green rooms behind.

From the plays that have survived it can be seen that no scenery was needed except a painted or embroidered curtain at the back of the stage which curiously was described by the Sanskrit word for 'Ionian' or 'Greek'. The characters in the plays provide the Rasa – or atmosphere, vividly describing the time, the place and the action as it proceeds. This characteristic was bequeathed to the Chinese theatre during the eleventh century.

13

CHINA

The roots of the Chinese theatre go far back into antiquity, but it was not till the widening of the Empire brought contact with India that dialogue was added to song and dance. The earliest permanent theatres were the temple stages: high platforms of brick and stone, with posts supporting and elaborately tiled roof. Later the private and court theatres copied this form, and improved it by adding trap-doors and galleries.

The popular theatre, however, was a much simpler erection of bamboo poles supporting planks hung with matting, which could be put up and dismantled in a few hours. These travelling theatres were carried round the country by touring companies giving performances at village festivals, often setting up the stage on the dry bed of a river.

The permanent public theatres in the cities grew up in the ch'a yüan or tea garden. The stage was square and set at the end of a rectangular courtyard surrounded by two verandahs, one above the other. These tea gardens developed in the seventeenth century and in function were very similar to the open-air Elizabethan playhouses.

The famous Pekin Opera of today performs in a modern Westernized theatre, though its repertoire contains many scenes and sequences from the classical period. The settings are formal, the costumes sumptuous and the make-ups which resemble masks are traditional.

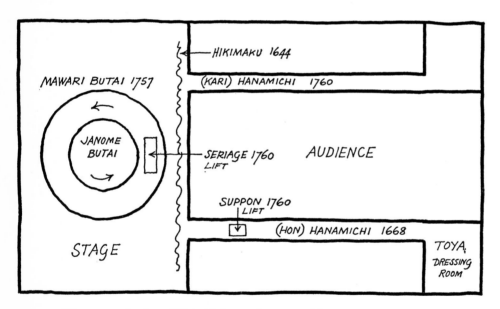

FIG 5   Diagrammatic plan of Kabuki theatre (not to scale)

JAPAN

The No-play of Japan is the only example of medieval theatre surviving intact. The playhouse is absolutely formal. The stage, about 20 ft square, is placed on the right-hand side of the audience. At each corner there is a pillar supporting an elaborate roof – a relic of the original outdoor playhouse. The chorus sit to the right of the stage and the orchestra of flute and drums sit behind stage in the Atoza. From here there is a walk, with roof and balustrade, leading to the actors' green room to the left of the audience. This walk along which the actors make their entrances is known as the Hashigarkari. The stage decoration for the No-play consists of a pine tree painted at the back of the stage, and three pine branches on the balustrade of the hashigarkari. The original significance of these is not known.

In contrast to the austere formality of the No-stage, the popular Kabuki theatre has developed a much more spectacular appeal. It is said to have originated in 1603 when a young maiden called Okuni, who served in a shrine at Izumo, went to Kyoto and gave a performance of dancing on the dry bed of the river Kamo. It was an adaptation of a ceremonial Buddhist dance, accompanied by flute and drum, and was an immediate popular success. She got together a group of pupils and formed a company which became known as Okuni's Kabuki. They built a playhouse based on the No-stage and developed a form of dance drama with singing, adapting the ritual of the No-play and later drawing on the material of the puppet theatre, Ningo Shibai.

From this time Japanese culture was entirely cut off from the rest of the world for two and a half centuries, and the Kabuki technique developed without any outside influences. A front curtain called the Hikimaku was introduced in 1644; a second curtain, the Kariotoshi, was designed to reveal or conceal an upstage setting. The actors' green room was moved to the back of the auditorium in 1668, and the walk to the stage was consequently made to pass through the spectators on the left-hand side of the house. It is known as the Hanamichi, and has been copied by Western theatres as a 'flower walk' in revue.

The revolving stage, Mawari Butai, was invented by the Japanese in 1757, for rapid and spectacular scene changes; and an inner revolve was added later, so that effects like a boat passing under a bridge could be achieved. Mechanical stage lifts were put in the outer revolve and in the hanamichi about 1760. All of these inventions were hand operated till the turn of this century.

2 Middle distance

MANY MANSIONS

'In my Father's house are many mansions; if it were not so I would have told you.' Thus William Tyndale translated St John's Gospel in 1525. These words could well apply to the re-enactment of the Easter story. A Mansion was the medieval name for a small platform stage on which part of a bible story was acted, originally in a church – the house of God.

During the ninth century the clergy had started to introduce short passages of dialogue into the celebration of the Easter Mass. The idea had caught on, and soon little plays were being written, not only on the Passion but on the Nativity, stories of the saints and lively sequences from the Old Testament. These 'Miracle' plays were first acted in a series of mansions arranged inside a church. But in the thirteenth century the clergy were forbidden to take part in the plays, so the local Guilds of craftsmen took charge and arranged the cycles of miracle plays out of doors.

Each town developed its own technique of presentation, but the mansions were used by all. A movable mansion was called a Pageant, and was drawn on wheels. The actors repeated their plays at a sequence of stations about the town. This was probably done at Chester and at York. It has been suggested that in Cornwall the cycle was played in a circular arena with mansions on the perimeter between blocks of spectators. The actors would have descended from the mansions and acted in the arena. In Wakefield there was a large fixed stage with the mansions placed about it. The Coventry Cycle possibly toured through several towns, which suggests the use of pageants.

These pageants and mansions were by no means naïvely designed, any more than the acting was crude. Rehearsing the actors, building and painting the decorations, and organizing (at York) forty-eight pageants arriving at the right stations on time, required great dexterity. The design of the pageants must have varied considerably – not only from play to play, but from town to town – governed by the width of the streets through which they had to pass. The simplest kind of pageant would have been a mansion mounted on a cart – say a throne on a daïs, with four pillars and a canopy. The cart would be surrounded by drapery to conceal actors doing a quick change between the axles, or using a trapdoor. When Lucifer falls from grace, the drapery opens and he is seen in Hell below.

The York Cycle was lately revived by E. Martin Browne in the Abbey ruins at York with professional actors and magnificent lighting. Amateurs and schools today often perform plays out of the five great cycles, which can be treated by the designer in many different ways: out of doors in a garden, courtyard or ruin, indoors in a church, a hall or even a theatre.

The best examples of the fixed stage for the Miracle plays are to be found in the records at Valenciennes (1547) and at Lucerne (1583), where no doubt the tradition had remained the same for generations. The Valenciennes fixed stage or *Décor Simultanée* consisted of many mansions set up on a high platform in the square. From left to right are Paradise, a Temple, Jerusalem, a Castle, the House of Bishops, the Golden Gate, the Prison. In front of the last two is a lake with a ship,

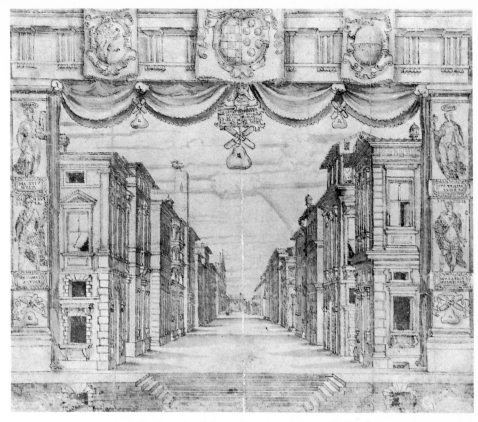

1 BARTOLOMEO NERONI (1500–73): *L'Ostensio* by Picolomini. Siena 1560.
Victoria and Albert Museum, London (Crown Copyright Reserved)

2 INIGO JONES (1573–1652): *Britannia Triumphans* by Sir William Davenant. London 1638.
Devonshire Collection, Chatsworth. Reproduced by permission of the Trustees of the Chatsworth Settlement

3 INIGO JONES: *Chloridia* by Ben Jonson. London 1631.
Devonshire Collection, Chatsworth. Reproduced by permission of the Trustees of the Chatsworth Settlement

4 FERDINANDO GALLI DA BIBIENA (1657–1745): Sketch.
Victoria and Albert Museum, London (Crown Copyright Reserved)

5 ANON: *The Empress of Morocco* by Elkanah Settle.
Showing the proscenium of the Dorset Garden Theatre, London 1673.
Victoria and Albert Museum, London (Crown Copyright Reserved)

6 FILIPPO JUVARRA (1685–1736): Setting for Cardinal Ottoboni's private theatre. Rome *c.* 1710.
Victoria and Albert Museum, London (Crown Copyright Reserved)

7 SIR JAMES THORNHILL (1675–1734): *Arsinoe, Queen of Cyprus* by Peter Motteux. London 1705.
Victoria and Albert Museum, London (Crown Copyright Reserved)

8 GUISEPPE GALLI DA BIBIENA (1696–1757): Sketch.
Victoria and Albert Museum, London (Crown Copyright Reserved)

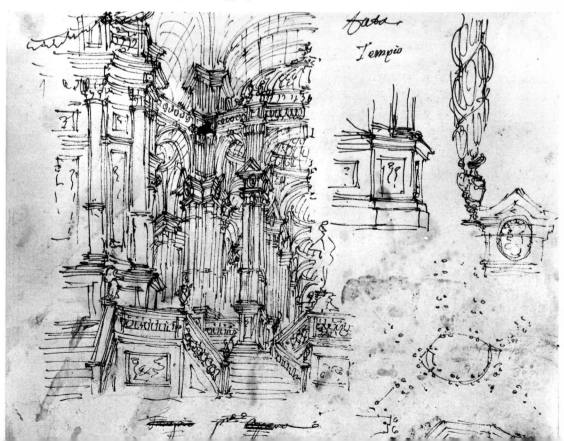

9 PHILIP JAMES DE LOUTHERBOURG (1740–1812):
Painting of David Garrick in *The Chances* by John Fletcher, adapted by Garrick. 1773.
Victoria and Albert Museum, London (Crown Copyright Reserved)

10 PHILIP JAMES DE LOUTHERBOURG: Model of Prison Scene.
Victoria and Albert Museum, London (Crown Copyright Reserved)

11 WILLIAM CAPON (1757–1827): *Richard III*. Backscene, Bosworth Field.
Reproduced by permission of the City of Leicester, Municipal Library

12 F. LLOYDS: *Macbeth*. For Charles Kean, 1853.
Victoria and Albert Museum, London (Crown Copyright Reserved)

13 H. CUTHBERT: *Macbeth*. For Charles Kean, 1853.
Victoria and Albert Museum, London (Crown Copyright Reserved)

14 WILLIAM TELBIN (1813–73): *The Tempest*. For Charles Kean, 1853.
Victoria and Albert Museum, London (Crown Copyright Reserved)

and at the extreme right is the Hell mouth with torture house above. Devils are coming out of the Hell mouth – which can evidently open and close. Above is the wheel of fire, and there is a good deal of smoke (see fig 6).

The Lucerne Easter play was arranged differently. The mansions were placed along the side of a rectangular market place. The plays took two days to perform, and the mansions were modified for the second day.

It will be seen that the designer had enormous scope for imagination in presenting the Miracle plays – but from their very nature a unified setting had not yet been contemplated: the plays had grown like crystals, but each was considered a separate entity and had a mansion to itself. A designer today would select and unify a sequence within a permanent setting, by isolating areas and lighting others – or by resetting parts of the set while the attention of the audience was elsewhere. The permanent set for the Oberammergau Passion is an example of how a fixed stage can be used in terms of modern design and lighting.

FIG 6   The Mansions at Valenciennes

Miracle plays continued in Europe after the Reformation, but another kind of work had begun to emerge which was not concerned with Bible stories, but with allegories of man's estate. These plays are known as Moralities, and need not concern us save to remark that from the designers' point of view the action is much more concentrated, and time and place less diffused. As the characters are symbolical, so is the setting – a street, a house, a castle or cathedral steps can represent the world in which mankind lives and dies. The designer today is equally unfettered – a modern everyman can live and die in a shack as well as in a skyscraper. He can also die in a proscenium frame, on an open stage or in the round. In fact the first known morality, *The Castle of Perseverance*, was played in the round in 1425 (see fig 7). The audience clearly sat round the stage, with scaffolds on the perimeter and the castle as a centre-piece. This kind of design has not been used to my knowledge in recent years, but is worthy of study, as what the audience can imagine

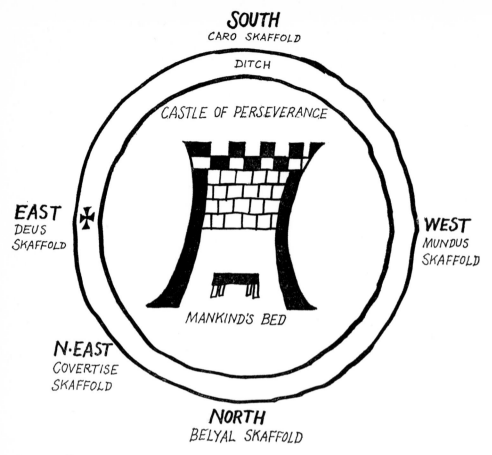

SOUTH
CARO SKAFFOLD

DITCH

CASTLE OF PERSEVERANCE

EAST
DEUS
SKAFFOLD

WEST
MUNDUS
SKAFFOLD

MANKIND'S BED

N·EAST
COVERTISE
SKAFFOLD

NORTH
BELYAL SKAFFOLD

FIG 7 Fifteenth-century design for *The Castle of Perseverance*, showing Mansions on perimeter

beside them and behind them is just as important as what they see in front of them, when a production is designed in the round – for what is behind one part of the audience faces another part.

INTERLUDE

A word must be said about the Interlude, which was an entertainment performed between the courses of a banquet. There is no reason to suppose that any stage platform would have been needed, as the audience were seated at long tables leaving a large rectangular space in the centre of the dining hall. A great deal of care was lavished on the actors' costumes; and as most of the interludes have small casts of actors there would have been little problem of 'masking' – one actor blotting out another – which is one of the difficulties of theatre in the round when the audience is on the same level as the actor.

THE RENAISSANCE

Towards the middle of the fifteenth century the Italians began to rediscover the mass of classical literature which they had inherited and which had been ignored for hundreds of years. After the invention of movable type in Germany, printing

FIG 8 Woodcuts from the edition of Terence published in Lyons 1493
Victoria and Albert Museum, London (Crown Copyright)

presses sprang up all over Europe, and the New Learning became available to all who could read. The architects and painters applied themselves to the rediscovered laws of geometry, mathematics and perspective.

For the first time the designer was in charge of the theatre. The old Roman plays were revived in court and palace – stages had to be built. Gradually the intermezzi between the acts of a play became more important than the play itself: first opera then ballet evolved. The architect-designer became responsible not only for erecting theatres in the great halls of Italian palaces, but for the invention of machines to change his scenery.

One such architect was Sebastian Serlio (1475–1554) who designed several theatres – including of course the scenery – and who wrote the first account of Renaissance theatre practice. The custom was to construct a steeply stepped auditorium, semicircular in form. The audience looked down on a wide flat stage

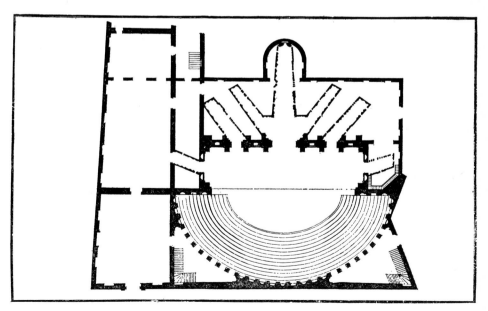

FIG 9 Plan of Teatro Olimpico, Vicenza 1584

27

on which the action took place, and *behind* which was a sloping stage where the scenery was built in perspective. Serlio designed three formal settings for the Tragic, the Comic and the Satyric types of entertainment, and these were to influence designers for many years. Plate 1 shows a design by Bartolomeo Neroni which follows Serlio's Tragic Scene very closely.

FIG 10   Section of Teatro Olimpico, Vicenza 1584

The first permanent theatre in Italy was the Teatro Olimpico at Vicenza. It was designed by Andrea Palladio, and finished by his son in 1584, with the help of Vincenzo Scamozzi, who added the magnificent vistas of houses in false perspective that can be seen through the arches at the back and sides of the stage; for the theatre still stands, perfectly expressing the transition from the ancient to the modern theatre (see figs 9 and 10).

PUBLIC THEATRES

Curiously, before the first theatre was built in Renaissance Italy, there were already public playhouses in London and Madrid. The Spanish actors played in Corrales or courtyards, with a platform stage at one end curtained at the back by a Manta. The audience stood in the courtyard or looked on from windows and balconies. There was no scenery. The first 'professional' theatre in Madrid was the Corral de la Cruz, opened in 1579.

The honour of building the first permanent public playhouse in Europe since Roman times, however, must go to James Burbage of London, who erected 'The Theatre', as it was simply called, on Finsbury Fields in 1576. The size and proportions of the building can only be guessed, as no description has come down to us; but in 1597 the lease was terminated and Burbage's two sons, Cuthbert and Richard, pulled down The Theatre, transported its timbers across the Thames and with them built The Globe. This famous playhouse was opened in 1599 by the Chamberlain's Men – the shareholding company of which Shakespeare was a member and Richard Burbage the leading actor. Again we have no builder's contract or description of the theatre, but there are several views of London, drawn and engraved before 1644, which show that the outside of the building was either round or polygonal. Shakespeare described it as a wooden 'O'.

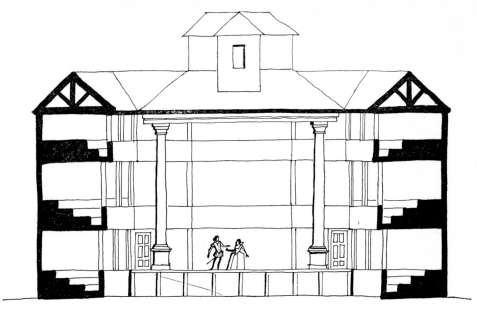

FIG 11a Conjectural section of an Elizabethan playhouse, 1570–1600

Now comes the fascinating part of the story: the Chamberlain's Men at the Globe were so successful that a rival company *copied* the building – constructing The Fortune in Cripplegate for the Lord Admiral's Men. The builder's contract for this enterprise has survived and from it we can conjecture at the plans of the Globe. The contract, which runs into some fifteen hundred words, mentions the 'newe errected house called the Globe' as a prototype for the builder, Peeter Streete, to copy – with one vital difference: that the frame of the Fortune was to be 'sett square'. As we have seen that the Globe was round or polygonal, it is possible to attempt a reconstruction of the Globe by using the measurements of the Fortune (see fig 11b).

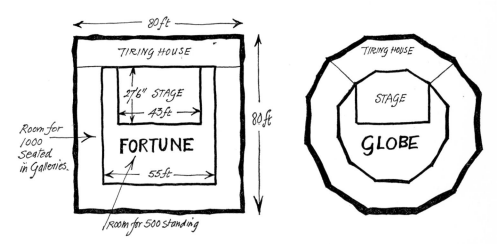

FIG 11b Plan of the known dimensions of the Fortune Theatre, 1600 and conjectural plan of Globe Theatre, 1599. This type of playhouse could comfortably accommodate 1,500 spectators with no one further than fifty-five feet from the centre of the stage. Absolute capacity would be 2,000

29

Probably no scenery was used on these stages except the significant or functional piece – a tub for Diogenes, a brazen head for Friar Bacon, an arbour in which to hang poor Horatio in *The Spanish Tragedy*, a well for Huanebango in the *Old Wives' Tale*, scaling ladders for an assault, rope ladders for ship boys and of course a trapdoor for Mephistopheles.

Companies were formed by shareholding actors who each had an interest in the company, under the patronage of the Chamberlain and the Lord Admiral. There were also the Boy Players from the great choir schools. All these companies were quite adaptable enough to play in any hall, inn yard, bear pit or bull ring in which they found themselves. But Burbage's theatre did not only grow out of the happy marriage of an inn yard with a bull ring; it also grew from a conscious intention to recreate the classical or Roman theatre – very little was known about the Greek theatre at this date, but some Roman arenas were still standing in Europe, as they are to this day. Modern copies of Elizabethan stages have shown how perfectly the form was suited to these plays, and, unexpectedly, to some modern plays as well.

Apart from the great open stages, there were the Private Theatres where the companies were able to play indoors in London during the winter and probably in poor weather during the rest of the year. It seems likely that some form of scenery could have been used in the indoor theatres.

THE MASQUE

While the dramatists were taking charge of the great open stages in England and Spain, the designers were very much in control of entertainments in the courts of Europe. The Revel's office accounts in England during the sixteenth century refer to 'Great Cloths', 'frames for the players' houses', and 'canvas to cover . . . other devices and clowds'. 'Clowds' were to become increasingly popular in the seventeenth century.

In Florence, Bernardo Buontalenti (1536–1608) worked tirelessly for the Medici family designing many intermezzi and founding a school of designers. The great English architect and designer, Inigo Jones (1573–1652), though not a pupil, was clearly influenced by the Buontalenti school on his visits to Italy. It is interesting to compare his London street scene (plate 2) with Neroni's design above.

In 1604 Inigo Jones became attached to the Court of James I and took complete control of the masques at Court. In form the masque was originally a primitive ceremony in which disguised dancers interrupted a banquet, presenting gifts to the noble visitor who was being feasted. The company then all joined together in a ceremonial dance. In time the entertainment became more sophisticated. Singing, and eventually dialogue, were introduced. The form was entirely allegorical and undramatic, as the purpose was to pay courtesy and honour to a visiting monarch, or to celebrate a royal wedding.

Ben Jonson was Court Poet in 1603, and to start with worked in close harmony with Inigo Jones. Their first collaboration was in *The Masque of Blackness*, 1605. Jonson describes the spectacle: 'An Artificial Sea . . . raised with waves, which seemed to move and in some places the billow to break, as imitating that orderly disorder, which is common in Nature. . . . The Masquers were placed in a great concave shell, like mother of pearle, curiously made to move on those waters and rise with the billow. . . . On the sides of the shell, did swim six huge sea monsters, varied in their shapes and dispositions, so that the backs of some were seen; some in purfle (profile), or side; others in face; and all having their lights burning out of whelks, or murex shells. These thus presented, the scene behind seemed a vast sea . . . which decorum made it more conspicuous and caught the eye afar off with a wandering beauty. . . . So much for the bodily part. Which was of master Ynigo Jones his design and act.'

There are several ways in which the artificial sea could have been made – all certainly known to Inigo Jones. One way is for a series of long, low, flat pieces of scenery, called ground rows, to be placed across the stage at intervals from the front to the back. They would have waved edges and be painted sea colour. Directly behind these would be another series, with waves painted in foam. The second series would be raised and lowered rhythmically by stage hands from the sides of the stage or from below. The effect of the waves would be to make the great concave shell appear to rise and fall, if it was built on a fixed platform between waves. The shell itself could be made to rise and fall by means of a lift operated by winches from below the stage. The sea monsters of course swam laterally between the waves – whether they were facing the audience or 'in purfle'. Another way of making waves was to nail pieces of board painted suitably to a shaft which was then revolved on spindles at the sides of the stage like a roast spit. A wavy cylinder was also used, but this was more complicated to construct.

For scene changes, the wing flats at the sides of the stage were arranged in groups so that they could be replaced by sliding in other flats when they were withdrawn. The back scene was divided in half, and similarly could be slid out and replaced by another pair of shutters, as they were called.

The hanging scenery above the stage that we now call borders was usually painted as 'Clowds', but there were other clouds that could be drawn across the stage on pulleys, to effect a transformation. Even more spectacular was the Glory, when the clouds were racked across the stage to reveal the gods above.

> 'The cloud capp'd towers, the gorgeous palaces,
> The solemn temples, the great globe itself.
> Yea, all that it inherit, shall dissolve,
> And like this insubstantial pageant faded,
> Leave not a rack behind.'

Everyone knows these lines from the *Tempest*, but not everyone realizes that they are an exact and technical description of the Jacobean masque, and of the magical and transitory art of Inigo Jones.

3 Foreground

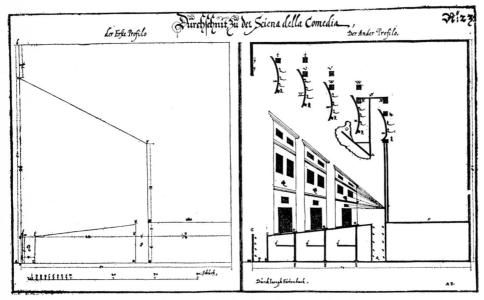

FIG 12 Joseph Furttenbach (1591–1667): Section of a stage showing perspective wings

Nicola Sabbattini was an exact contemporary of Inigo Jones, and he wrote a practical book on theatre machines and scenery which was published in 1638. It is much fuller than Serlio's and had a great influence on designers throughout Europe. He lays down the method of building a stage in great detail – showing how perspective should be used and how the scene should be lit. He also describes the way that the audience should be best accommodated: 'Care should be taken always to place the most beautiful ladies in the middle so that those who are acting . . . perform more gaily, with greater assurance and with greater zest.'

His second book describes methods of changing scenery. Two of these devices, that were to remain in use in the theatre for over three hundred years, were described in the last chapter – the back shutters and the grooves for the side wings. Other methods of scene change which Sabbattini discusses are: painted cloths that can be slid across the faces of the wings, by means of a stick held by a stage hand; frames hidden behind the wing returns which can be slid upstage and conceal the second wing; finally the triangular wing piece – like the Greek periaktoi – painted differently on each facet. When these prisms were turned a new scene was revealed. He also explains the construction of trapdoors, fountains, how to bring on a ship and turn it round, how to lower a cloud with persons on it from the back of the sky to the front of the stage, and how to make a paradise. Among his more delightful chapters are 'How to show the whole scene in flames . . . to be avoided as much as possible on account of the danger sometimes attendant upon it'. His clear explanations and simple diagrams are of incalculable value, and have been inherited unwittingly by all stage carpenters and designers.

Another important early writer on practical designing was Joseph Furttenbach, who studied in Italy before returning to Germany in the sixteen-twenties where he pursued a long and successful career as engineer, architect, stage designer and writer. When he was seventeen he had been captivated by Parigi's designs for the Medici wedding festivals in 1608: 'At the end of the act the whole scene changes into a pleasure garden, a sea, a wood, or some other place, with such dexterity that those who are watching cannot see the change and think they have lost their senses.' Bearing in mind the novelty of the spectacle, the ingenuity of the devices for scene changing and the flattering unction of candlelight, the enthusiasm of Furttenbach was not as wild as it may appear to us now – used as we are to film dissolves and television mixes. The scene change was magical then in candlelight – it can still hold the old magic today in electric light, given knowledge of the old magic.

BAROQUE

In Italy and France the enthusiasm for the theatre of illusion and of spectacle had led to a diminished interest in the drama and an increase of interest in the proliferation of design for opera and ballet. Architects began to specialize in designing scenery. It was very profitable. Vast opera houses were being constructed by princes all over Europe to keep up with the other princes. It is an arguable point whether the building of opera houses is more conducive to the harmony of humanity than the making of nuclear bombs, but in the seventeenth century rivalry was confined to the explosion of new scenic devices. Giacomo Torelli was the first artist to specialize in designing scenery; some of his effects were so astute that it was rumoured in Venice that he was in league with the devil, which shows the power of the dedicated designer.

The form of the opera house varied considerably. Emerging as it did from the temporary court theatres, the dominant factor to start with was still the royal or princely 'State' – a platform placed in the centre, with the best view of the perspective. The Intermezzi were performed on the wide shallow stage in front of the scenery, and the ballets or dancing took place on the flat floor of the auditorium between the stage and the state box. The earliest auditorium which satisfied both these requirements was designed by Giambattista Aleotti (1546–1636), who built the Teatro Farnese at Parma in 1618 (see fig 13).

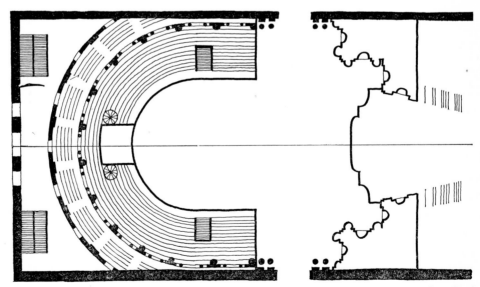

FIG 13   Teatro Farnese at Parma, designed by Aleotti, 1618. Redrawn from *Encyclopédie* of Diderot and D'Alembert, 1772

33

Architects tried many modifications, to satisfy sightlines and acoustics. The horseshoe plan eventually proved the most effective. When the stages grew larger and the box office more clamorous, the dancing floor became raked for seating, on benches. A typical feature of the Baroque playhouse was a tier of boxes surrounding the auditorium. This satisfied both acoustics and class distinction.

The seventeenth century saw the foundation of dynasties of Italian scenic designers – the Galli and the Galliari families spread over the whole of Europe, designing opera houses, stage machinery and settings. Ferdinando Galli da Bibiena (1657—1743) broke the tradition of straight perspective scenery with the vanishing point in the centre, and was the first artist to use 'diagonal perspective', employing two vanishing points (see fig 14 and plate 4). His sons Giuseppe and Antonio worked in Germany (see plate 8), and his grandson Carlo designed the sumptuous interior of the opera house at Bayreuth which is still to be seen. In fact the Galli family invaded the whole continent of Europe with their rich baroque designs till almost the end of the eighteenth century. The Galliari family from Piedmont had an equally illustrious history.

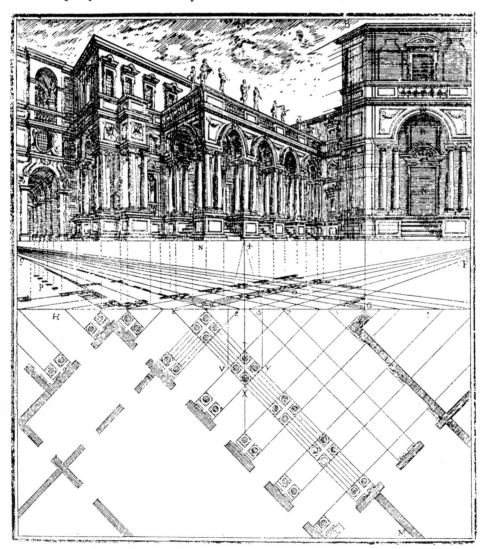

FIG 14 Design by Ferdinando Galli da Bibiena, the innovator of diagonal perspective

In England, eighteen years of Commonwealth rule had put an end to all but private performances of plays, and prevented the masque from growing into an indigenous form of opera. Four years before Charles II was restored to the throne in 1660, Sir William Davenant had brought out *The Seige of Rhodes* at Rutland House in London. This work, known as the first English opera, was mounted by John Webb, a pupil of Inigo Jones. Designs for the scenery have survived, showing four permanent wings, and sets of back shutters. This system was to become common practice, with stock sets of wings and shutters doing service for: The Mall, Covent Garden, St James's Park, together with suitable (or unsuitable) interior domestic scenes, palaces, temples and, of course, prisons.

The lighting was achieved by suspended chandeliers in the auditorium and over the stage. Footlights consisting of a row of candles are known to have been used in France before 1600, but by 1670 wicks floating in oil seem to have been more common. To this day footlights are often still called 'floats'. With flat painting and visible sources of lighting, the effect of the scenery was entirely due to the skill of the painter and that of the carpenter who had constructed the grooves for changing the wings and shutters.

ROMANTICISM

The reaction against the Baroque in the theatre took the form of a refined neo-classicism in architecture coupled with highly romantic landscaping: mountain scenes with pine trees, rocky gorges and caverns, stormy skies and flashes of lightning which might reveal a crouched figure sheltering under a blasted oak.

In Paris Jean Nicholas Servandony (1695–1766) created new effects of lighting, spectacle and transformation scenes by using gauzes and transparencies lit from behind. The great English actor David Garrick visited the Paris Opera, seeking to improve the lighting at Drury Lane in London. In 1771 he engaged the services of Philip James de Loutherbourg (1740–1810) already known in Paris as a romantic landscape painter, paying him the colossal sum of £500 a year. Garrick and de Loutherbourg made revolutionary changes at Drury Lane. Abolishing the old chandeliers over the stage, they hid the lighting behind the proscenium. This had two far-reaching effects; first it forced the actor upstage behind the frame, second it made possible a new kind of scenic illusion – particularly for exterior scenes, as the sources of lighting were hidden. But de Loutherbourg went further than this. Delighting in fog, mist, shifting clouds and shafts of moonlight – not to mention fire, volcanoes, rain, tempest and torrent, he contrived changeable light effects by means of stained or painted silks through which he projected light from the wings. The reproduction of one of his paintings shows the sort of effect he achieved (see plate 9). A cut-out piece from one of his models shows an interior scene (see plate 10). De Loutherbourg was certainly a great innovator of 'naturalism' in the illusionist theatre, but he dealt only with flat painted surfaces – whether opaque or transparent, and was never much concerned with anything more three-dimensional than a flight of steps.

The next development in England was a lust for antiquarian accuracy in scenic design. This was coupled with the Gothic revival in architecture and literature. William Capon (1757–1827) designed scenery for Drury Lane and Covent Garden, for revivals of Shakespeare and historical dramas. His scenery for *Hamlet* and *Richard III* was probably used by the great actor Edmund Kean (see plate 11, which shows his design for the tents of the rival armies before the battle of Bosworth).

It must be mentioned here that it was not the custom in nineteenth-century

England for one designer to prepare all the scenes of a play. As many as six painter-designers were sometimes employed on one production. The pairs of wings and shutters went into the stock of the theatre and often reappeared in productions of other plays.

GASLIGHT

The theatre of illusion was immeasurably enhanced by the introduction of gaslight, which could be controlled from a distance at the turn of a cock. The two main theatres in London were equipped with gaslighting in 1817, on the stage and in the auditorium – with the double advantage of control both sides of the curtain. The audience could be darkened at will and the stage lighting balanced as never before.

For the next sixty years many fine designers painted scenes to be lit by this subtle, soft, glowing light – so marvellous for cloths and transformations. The Grieve family – like the Gallis – invented scenic designs for three generations (see plate 15); the Telbin family were still painting scenery in this century. Work by F. Lloyds and H. Cuthbert is well worth studying as fine examples of design in the eighteen-fifties (see plates 12 and 13). William Telbin (1813–1873) painted for Macready and for Irving (see plate 14). Most often employed by Irving was Hawes Craven (1837–1910) who had the theatre in his bones and paint in his finger tips. His sketches for *Macbeth* at the Lyceum in 1888 show his feeling for atmosphere and power as a designer (see plates 17 and 18).

NATURALISM

Meanwhile the romantic school of design was being undermined by the growing demand for naturalism in the theatre, first with Tom Robertson's plays at the Prince of Wales Theatre in London, then with Ibsen's plays in Norway, the Duke of Saxe-Meiningen's productions in Germany, Antoine's in Paris, Strindberg's in Sweden, Stanislavsky's in Moscow and finally Belasco's in New York. All these writers and directors required their designers to throw away the clichés of the romantic theatre and to concentrate on naturalistic detail. One of the results of this attitude was the invention of the box set for interior scenes.

In the romantic theatre, scenery had basically consisted of wings running parallel to the footlights, borders above the stage from wing to wing, and backcloths or drops which had replaced the shutters during the nineteenth century. Sometimes the wing flats had additional flats hinged or lashed to them (see chapter 5). These 'return' flats, as they are called, were set at an angle and ran upstage. This system had been in use since the time of Serlio, and it meant that every interior scene had to consist of a series of sections of wall leading up to the shutters or cloth. The box set abolished this system and enclosed the stage with flats running up and down-stage on both sides – meeting a solid wall of flats at the back. By this means three sides of a seemingly realistic room could be achieved, with doors and windows placed where required instead of between the wing flats.

Tom Robertson was the eldest of twenty-two children of an actor. He became a dramatist after a career as an actor, scene painter and song writer. When he brought out his plays at the Prince of Wales theatre in the eighteen-sixties he insisted on real walls with real doors with real door handles – and got them. It was a revolution.

In Germany in the eighteen-eighties the Duke of Saxe-Meiningen insisted on another aspect of naturalism. An artist himself, he designed not only the scenery and costumes, but the whole plan of movement for his productions. In integrating the action with the setting he became the progenitor of the modern director.

When Strindberg published *Miss Julie* in 1888, he wrote: 'Having only a single setting, one may expect it to be realistic; but nothing is harder than to get a room that looks like a room, however easily the painter can produce flaming volcanoes and water-falls. No doubt the walls must be canvas, but it really seems time to draw the line at painted shelves and pots and pans.'

In Paris André Antoine founded the Théâtre Libre for the purpose of producing the new naturalistic dramas of Ibsen, Strindberg, Hauptmann, Brieux and others. Like Robertson in London twenty years before, he made far-reaching reforms, getting rid of wings and borders and building solid settings.

The Moscow Art Theatre was founded just before the turn of the century by Konstantin Stanislavsky and Vladimir Nemirovich-Danchenko. Stanislavsky was an amateur actor who had come under the influence of Saxe-Meiningen's company; Danchenko had been professor of a drama course for some seven years when their historic meeting took place. Everyone knows the result. The Art Theatre was formed and a new system of acting, setting, direction, stage management and teaching was born. No detail was too small to be ignored – in any department. The same is true of the company today. Stanislavsky's profound penetration into the process by which an actor arrives at his truth has affected the art of the theatre throughout the world. Every born actor has had a method of work since acting began, but very few have been articulate or self-analytical enough to be able to describe their processes. Stanislavsky did this, and was also able to lay down a method of approach suitable to directors and designers at the same time. *A* method; not *the* method. Every designer – like every actor – must develop his own method of work.

It was Nemirovich-Danchenko's encouragement of Chechov that gave Stanislavsky and his designers an entirely new attitude towards naturalism in scenic design. Like Robertson's preoccupation with door-handles and Strindberg's desire for a room to look like a room, Chechov's characters had to live in houses that looked like houses – not flapping canvas – with birches outside the porch, and a lake with the moon rising beyond, a town on fire or a cherry orchard outside stretching for acres around the house. Chechov made his designers think of more than a room: he made them think of people in a house and the town or countryside beyond. How this can best be done in the theatre now is a point to which we will return, but in the nineteen-hundreds the demand was for naturalism to the smallest detail. This meant solid sets with solid doors, solid birch trees with solid leaves. Only within this solid framework could the actor behave naturalistically – as in life. The designer had ceased to be a romantic painter and returned momentarily to his original function as an architect and interior decorator, with occasional landscape gardening thrown in.

CRAIG

Edward Gordon Craig was a young actor at the Lyceum theatre in London when he decided to leave Irving's company and form his own. For a while he published woodcuts and lithographs; then in 1900 he started to design and direct plays. In 1905 he published his first book, *The Art of the Theatre*, written in the form of a dialogue between the playgoer and the stage director. He developed his ideas in a much longer book, *On the Art of the Theatre*, six years later, which has run into many editions, and at least eight translations appeared before 1924. Many of his designs have been shown and reproduced since, and there is no serious director or designer who has not benefited directly or indirectly from Craig's ideas.

We have seen how Serlio and his followers applied the principles of the ancient to the Renaissance theatre and how the spectacular school of Baroque designers developed. We have seen how the romantic ideals of the eighteenth century reacted against the Baroque and how, in its turn, the naturalistic theatre was a swing away from the romantic.

Craig released the designer from the shackles of naturalism by showing that the implication is more forceful than the statement. To the impressionist painter the suggestion of a solid was more important than the actual delineation of its shape. In Craig's designs light plays across surfaces and is reflected off them – the structure of the setting becomes a vehicle for the interplay of light and shadow which creates the atmosphere of the scene. During the eighteen-eighties electric lighting had replaced gaslight in the main theatres throughout the world. Craig's effects are all conceived in relation to lighting direction, diffusion or concentration. This could not have been achieved by gaslight. Craig's designs and writings should be studied and pondered over by every aspiring designer. Pure gold will be found on every page.

In Switzerland Adolphe Appia had also seized upon the potentiality of electric light, and his designs for the Wagner operas were revolutionary in their rejection of flat painted scenery in favour of the painting of light upon solid, three-dimensional shapes. It is one of the strange coincidences of life that Craig and Appia should have independently and simultaneously made similar discoveries which affected the whole future of scenic design and lighting. The two men did not meet till February 1914, in Zurich, where there was an international exhibition of scenic designs. Until that moment they had no first-hand knowledge of each other's work.

BETWEEN THE WARS

The work of serious designers between the wars shows a conflict of influences and experiments culminating in the Epic Theatre of Bertholt Brecht. To analyse these in detail is beyond the scope of this book. All these influences are still with us and are liable to overlap in any one designer's experience.

The influence of Craig and Appia in the simplification of setting has been paramount. Conflicting influences still with us are the old romanticism of the opera and the naturalism of Stanislavsky's designers.

Georg Fuchs in Munich and his designer Fritz Erler stood midway between Craig's three-dimensional symbolism and Saxe-Meiningen's historical naturalism.

Harley Granville-Barker in London dusted the cobwebs from the theatre and with his designers, Albert Rutherston and Norman Wilkinson, presented post-impressionist Shakespeare, in which the action of the play was allowed to advance continuously by means of a semi-permanent setting, with a front curtain which swept across the stage, leaving a large 'apron' or forestage in front. This method eliminated the old 'set scenes' of the nineteenth century, and their attendant delays involving heavy scene changes. It was an attempt to return to Shakespeare's playhouse.

Diaghilev's Russian ballet – at first a luscious romantic revival in the hands of Bakst and Benois – later encouraged painters to experiment with cubism and constructivism.

The horrors of the First World War, the Russian Revolution and, later, the Abyssinian War and the Spanish Civil War which foreshadowed the Second World War, were all inevitably reflected in the work of the artists of the period. Symbolism, Fauvism, Expressionism, Dadaism, Cubism, Surrealism and Vorticism were not labels to hide behind, but banners to advance.

The naturalism of the Moscow Art Theatre had both positive and negative results. Vsevolod Emilievich Meyerhold tried to develop a 'bio-mechanical' system of design, direction and acting, which never came to fruition. Alexander Yakovlevish

Tairov experimented with cubist and constructivist scenery, costumes and make-up. Eugene Vakhtangov, who joined the Art Theatre as a young actor and was afterwards put in charge of the studio attached, later made some striking non-naturalist productions, culminating in *The Dybbuk* for the Habima Theatre the year he died. Nikolai Pavlovich Okhlopkov studied under Meyerhold and became the director of the Realist Theatre – producing plays in a round arena, with constructivist designs. The positive influences of the Moscow Art Theatre were a result of the tours made in the early nineteen-twenties, when Europe and America first saw the perfection of the technique of the company, and a few years later when Stanislavsky's books were translated. The Group Theatre in New York in the nineteen-thirties owed its inspiration to the precepts of Stanislavsky and the Moscow Art Theatre.

In Germany Max Reinhardt directed every sort of play in every sort of style. Undeterred by physical limitations, he turned circuses into cathedrals and cathedrals into circuses. He was a master of mass movement, a connoisseur of detail, and somehow managed to combine a genius for the general with a precision for the particular. Many of his productions were designed by Ernst Stern. One of his disciples is Erwin Piscator, whose famous productions of the plays by Ernst Toller and the adaptation of *The Good Soldier Schweik* employed constructivist scenery – using film projections on screens, and a sliding 'treadmill' stage to make the action flow.

Bertholt Brecht (1878–1956), dramatist, poet, philosopher and director has been one of the most influential figures in the theatre since the nineteen-thirties. His development of the Epic Theatre – an eclectic combination of parable, propaganda, narrative and point numbers is now well known. Inseparable from Brecht's Epic Theatre is the *Verfremdungseffekte* – signifying the actor's device for contriving strangeness – referred to in English as the alienation effect. The actor here is not concerned with creating a realistic character and thus an illusion of life. He is concerned with instructing the audience about his character and situation without becoming emotionally involved. The naturalistic theatre is concerned with stimulating the emotions; epic theatre is concerned with examining them. This clearly calls for a special approach by the designer – beyond the individual style required by each play. Scenery is treated as large-scale properties; detail must be real and exact where the actor comes in contact with it – otherwise left out or implied. To use Brecht's words, 'Whatever does not further the narrative harms it'. Great care is lavished on surface and texture – whether of wood, metal, canvas or plaster. The framework is formal: curtains or wings with no borders above so that the stage lighting is in view. Screens are flown in from above upon which words, drawings or film can be projected. A large revolve brings on small built pieces in screen or skeletal form while the action continues.

The epic theatre brings us to today; but the naturalism of the box set, impressionism, romanticism and the baroque are all to be seen on the stage, and even a short list of important designers since 1945 would prove to be very long indeed. A selection of work is reproduced in the following pages. Readers would be well advised to refer to the many volumes of reproductions that have appeared over the last thirty years, some of which will be found listed at the end of this book.

Our next step is to investigate the practical approach to planning a production and the various methods of building scenery. I will deal with conventional professional practice, since it is only by knowing the rules that one can learn how to break them. This applies equally to a designer working in a church, village hall, repertory theatre or the largest opera house in the world.

4 Planning

Ideally, the scenic designer today should be historian, archaeologist and anti-quarian; architect, sculptor and painter; visionary and poet; an expert carpenter and electrician, with something of the engineer thrown in. Some experience as an actor – however trivial – is also invaluable. If the designer has an interest in or an affinity with these occupations all may be well. But more important than all this knowledge is the ability to discover the basic element of the play in hand.

PLAY READING

The first essential is to know how to read a play. This may sound simple, but it is not. Many actors are not able to read plays. They read parts, but not the whole. This is perhaps largely vanity, but the designer is vain too, and can get *illusions de grandeur* before even opening the script. The title of the play itself may provide an indication of plot only, and not of theme. *The Merchant of Venice*, for instance, is not primarily concerned with merchants or Venice, but with the subject of mercy and justice. Many titles of plays suggest visual images that do not necessarily suit the atmosphere of the scene; and a designer, if he is not careful, may quickly get off to a wrong start.

Theatre managers, directors and designers have to teach themselves how to read plays. To be able to interpret and visualize what the dramatist is *meaning* within what he is *saying* is a special craft. This may appear obvious; but the meaning itself is open to more than one interpretation, and the director's and designer's convictions must work in conjunction, or there will be no unity. You may be asked to design *The Merchant of Venice* by a director who believes the play is about anti-semitism, or usury. All aspects must be discussed. Remember that a play is not written to be read; it is only alive when acted. The misunderstanding of this simple fact has bedevilled literary criticism of drama for some few hundreds of years. A play means what it means in performance – and this depends both on the director and on the times in which it is performed.

The designer's business in reading and re-reading a play is twofold: to absorb the atmosphere with the inner eye, and the detail with the outer eye. Do not wait for the stage manager to come to you with a list of props. Note them all, for when Antony or Napoleon or General Grant is handed a map in act three it must be there, and it must be the right shape, colour and weight. It can only be so if it is seen as part of the whole in the first place.

We can return to detail later. But it must not be forgotten that everything seen on the stage is the designer's responsibility, from a candle to a flagpole. Very often the designer is also responsible for the costumes, but that is not now our concern.

First things first. The play is all that matters. Read it until it becomes a part of you; so that everything you see, hear and think becomes related to it – like a tune that you can't get out of your head. Do not think about flats and rostrums, or trucks and cycloramas. That will all come later, and anyhow you may end up with barbed wire and foam plastic.

15 THOMAS GRIEVE (1779–1882): *King Lear*. For Charles Kean, 1858.
Victoria and Albert Museum, London (Crown Copyright Reserved)

16 W. GORDON: *A Midsummer Night's Dream*. 1856.
Victoria and Albert Museum, London (Crown Copyright Reserved)

17/18
HENRY HAWES CRAVEN (1837–1910): *Macbeth*. Two sketches for Henry Irving.
Lyceum Theatre, London 1888.
Victoria and Albert Museum, London (Crown Copyright Reserved)

19 EDWARD GORDON CRAIG: *Hamlet.* 1910.
Photo: Victoria and Albert Museum. Copyright E. G. Craig

EDWARD GORDON CRAIG: *Hamlet*. Two models for Stanislavsky, Moscow Art Theatre, 1912.
Reproduced by permission of Edward A. Craig

22/23
EDWARD GORDON CRAIG: Above, Design for an Open Air Theatre;
Below, *Bethlehem* by Laurence Houseman. Imperial Institute, London, 1902.
Reproduced by permission of Edward A. Craig

24 VLADIMIR DIMITRIEV: *The Three Sisters* by Anton Chechov. Moscow Art Theatre, 1940.
Photo: Society for Cultural Relations with the USSR, London

25 VLADIMIR DIMITRIEV: *Uncle Vanya* by Anton Chechov. Moscow Art Theatre, 1947.
Photo: Society for Cultural Relations with the USSR, London

26 OLIVER MESSEL': *Idomeneo* by Giovanni Battista Varesco and Wolfgang Amadeus Mozart.
Model for Glyndebourne Opera, 1951.
Photo: Angus McBean

27 JAMES BAILEY: *A Midsummer Night's Dream.*
The Royal Shakespeare Theatre, Stratford upon Avon 1949.
Photo: W. Churcher

28 DONALD OENSLAGER: *Mary Stuart* by Friedrich Schiller. New York 1957

29 JOSEPH MIELZINER: *The Lark* by Jean Anouilh. New York 1955

When you have read the play you must do your research. This can involve museums, libraries, newspaper cuttings, gossip, art galleries, railway journeys – even concert halls and gramophone records. Some designers find music helpful in trying to 'smell out' the atmosphere of a play. Something intangible is often communicated by music, which adds another dimension to what one is doing. Listening to Dowland or Morley when preparing the production of an Elizabethan play may give the designer an insight which no amount of reading can provide. This is equally true for a modern play – whether it is Brubeck, Britten or the Beatles that helps the inner ear.

By research in a library or museum I do not mean to suggest wholesale shop-lifting. This is not always a short cut - and can be a very long way round. You may stumble on an appropriate description or picture that gives you a starting point, from which you and the director may decide that the whole production should be done – Brueghel, Daumier, for example. Remember, though, that you have still got to design it, draw it out, scale it up, build it and paint it before you are finished. During this process it will have become yours rather than Daumier's or Brueghel's because you will have had to digest and regurgitate all the impressions and discussions that must lead up to actually designing the scenes.

It is possible that you may not have to do any physical research. The play may take place in a naturalistic environment with which you are familiar down to the last detail. Curiously, this may prove more difficult than a subject that requires you to find out about the past or about a foreign country, or even to speculate about the future. Memory can inhibit imagination.

Moreover, a familiar background, which the director will no doubt tell you that you know like the back of your hand, will need a carefully balanced selection of detail, because you are bound to be emotionally involved. This does not mean that you should not be emotionally involved – you can't help it. But it is also necessary to acquire the ability to look at a play objectively, as it were, through a telescope; to find the disinterested passion that the greatest portrait painters have always had. And in addition to that, you must also have an underlying *reason* for everything you design.

When you have digested the play properly, when you have absorbed all that you can from the text (the background, middle distance, foreground and the purpose of the play), this is the time to re-discuss the matter with the director. The director has probably already indicated a line of approach, and this may have influenced you in your study. Do not think he has deprived you of your initiative; play production is a composite art, demanding involvement with many people. Sparks fly and ideas are germinated in discussion.

Your contact with the director throughout the early stages of planning is the most important element in shaping the form and atmosphere of the production. If designer and director have an outlook in common, know each other well and have done many plays together, they will talk and think in shorthand. But if not, there are no short cuts. The whole meaning and purpose of the play must be discussed in great detail, so that each one knows what is in the other's mind. Otherwise the result will be merely a commercial contract in which the designer is providing scenery by the yard. Getting a play on stage is very rarely the result of one person's effort. It might be so for someone like Saxe-Meiningen or Craig who is able to plan, design and direct without more than physical assistance. But this is rare. We are concerned here with the average situation that arises when a designer is asked to invent the scenery for a play.

Assuming that the director and the designer have by now both studied the play, let us examine the next stage through an actual example: an Old Vic production of Shakespeare's *Richard II* at the New Theatre, London in 1947. The director was Sir Ralph Richardson; Richard was Sir Alec Guinness; I was the designer.

Detailed discussions between director and designer were held over a long period (during lunches, cups of tea in *Cyrano de Bergerac* intervals and during *Alchemist* rehearsals). Finally the synthesis of ideas was subjected to the well-weighed comments of the leading actor, and the searching criticism of one of the directors of the company. The very experienced production stage manager, John Sullivan, had been advising throughout.

The initial springboard of the discussions had been this: the play is one with nineteen scenes of extremely varied locality – an easy job for the Elizabethans, but a problem to present as an organic whole to an audience used to permanent sets, changing sets, blackouts, front curtains concealing changes, and the whole gamut of designers' contrivances since Craig and Granville-Barker broke away from the Irving tradition.

I remember one early conversation during a *Cyrano de Bergerac* interval. It went something like this:

R.R.   I'm not sure how you're going to do this, but I have a strong feeling that the set should all be wood. All made of wood – perhaps moveable about the stage. You should be able to go in and out of it.

M.W.   Permanent for the whole play?

R.R.   Yes. But perhaps we could change it from time to time; move it back for the lists, close it for Gaunt, use a raised bit for Flint Castle, enclose it again for the deposition and bring it right downstage for the prison.

M.W.   We must have an upstairs for Flint Castle and probably for the lists too . . . this is leading us towards a formal structure, with an inner room, an outer stage and an upper stage. In fact Elizabethan.

R.R.   Why not?

M.W.   Costumes?

R.R.   Why not Elizabethan structure . . .

M.W.   With fourteenth-century costumes?

R.R.   Don't worry about that. The most important thing is that the actors should be at home on the set, which should be a prop they know and love. They must use it – handle it lovingly . . . so it should be made of beautiful wood.

M.W.   What sort of colour?

R.R.   (pause) Wood colour. The colour of beautiful wood . . . like . . . like this . . .

M.W.   Cedar.   (picking up a pencil).

R.R.   Make the whole set of wood.

M.W.   Homogeneous.

R.R.   That's a five dollar word.

M.W.   It won't be a five dollar set.

R.R.   Now go away dear chap and think about it. Do some sketches and we'll talk about it again. Remember . . . wood.

This conversation may seem delightfully vague, but in fact it precipitated the whole scene. The main ingredients of the plan had emerged from it – they then had to be crystallized on the backs of envelopes – scribbles in pencil, chalk or pen – as a search was made for one shape that would work. There were no drawings to scale yet, only the implied scale of the human body walking about the stage.

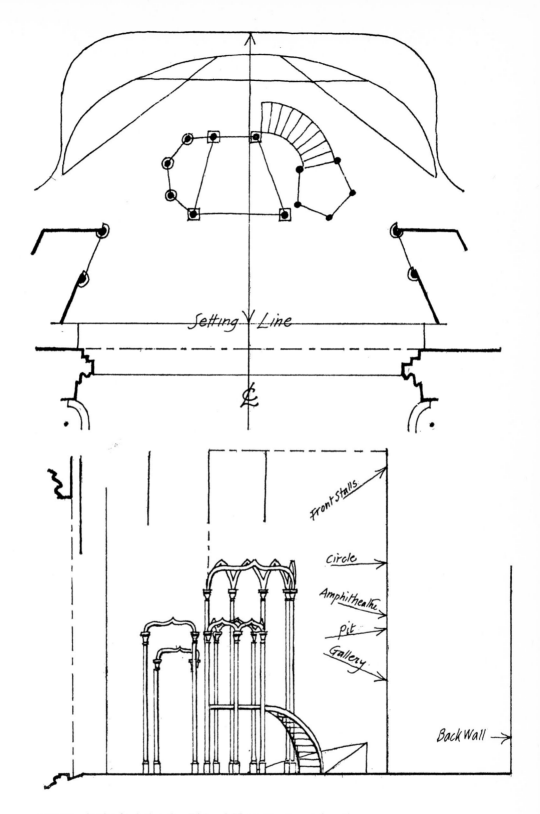

Setting Line

Front Stalls

Circle

Amphitheatre

pit

Gallery

Back Wall

FIG 15 Author's design for *Richard II*, 1947, plan and section

The idea of a mobile inner and upper stage proved to be more limiting than flexible, and we decided on a skeleton arrangement of columns, containing an upper platform and an inner acting area that could be filled in with low curtains in front, or panels behind. By cutting four scenes and allowing only one interval (after the surrender of Richard at Flint Castle), we were able to find two basic patterns: the first open to the sky, the second enclosed. Each pattern had six variations of its own, which achieved the maximum visual change with the minimum physical adjustment (see figs 15, 16 and plate 34).

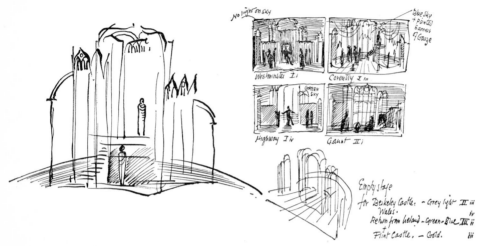

FIG 16   Author's rough sketches for *Richard II*, 1947

SKETCHES AND GROUND PLANS

It might be as well to elaborate here on the business of preliminary sketches. Most artists need to use line or line and tone, to clarify their minds over what they are thinking now and what they intend to do later in form and colour. A line drawing is like an armature waiting for clay (see fig 17).

It is also possible to make written notes of all the requirements of a scene, or series of scenes, and then to make a ground plan including everything noted. If you are in a hurry – and you usually are – this is a quick way to work, provided that you know with your inner eye what the elevation is going to look like and how to achieve it.

 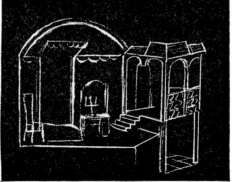

FIG 17   Rough sketches by Motley for *Romeo and Juliet*, 1935, showing half of the stage. Left: Balcony scene; right: Juliet's bedroom

There is a third method which many designers use. This is to start straight away with the model: in other words, to make your sketches in three dimensions. (For years I have not painted a flat design for a setting; I far prefer to work in solid from the start.) If you adopt this method, you not only miss out a step, but you can visualize the lighting objectively, rather than subjectively as in a painting or sketch. It does require experience, however, to make a sketch model without being inhibited by the scale.

I will return to models later. For the moment, it is important to realize that each of these methods is equally valid, so long as one remembers that communication and understanding in the early stages of planning are essential. You may find a director who is completely lost when he looks at a plan; you may find one who *only* wants a plan.

Another word about sketches: they may be attractive or formidable, delightful or awesome, but if you do not know how to carry out their implications when scaled up in three dimensions, lit, and acted in – they will remain merely sketches.

When a sketch or plan of the idea has been agreed in principle between director and designer – as a working hypothesis of how the play might be staged – the next step is to make the model. For this, begin by making your ground plan to scale, plotting exactly the positions of your various pieces of scenery. If you are working in a small or average sized theatre, half an inch to the foot (1 : 24) is a comfortable scale to work in. In the metric system, four centimetres to the metre (1 : 25) is the nearest equivalent. In a larger theatre, half this scale is easier to handle – a quarter of an inch to the foot or two centimetres to the metre.

If there are no plans of the theatre available, you must measure the stage yourself, taking careful note of any obstructions in the wings and backstage – iron supports or jutting brick walls that might get in the way, recesses that might prove useful. You must also take into account the sight-lines from the front of the house: from the widest rows, the lowest rows and the highest rows of seats.

Always mark the centre line of the stage on your plans and always find out if there is a customary setting line (in front of which no scenery should be placed) – and why. The setting line is a convenience for the stage carpenter of the theatre – related to the fall of the house curtain (or front tabs). You may not want to use the tabs – particularly if there is a large apron in front – in which case you must use your own discretion as to where you put the setting line; but it must be clearly shown in relationship to the architecture of the building. The centre line and the setting line make a right-angle on your plan, from which scenery and furniture can be set in any theatre.

Once a plan of the stage has been made or acquired (and, if necessary, you have worked out an average size stage for a tour), cut up a piece of blockboard, strengthen a piece of plywood with battens, or, if it is a very simple setting, simply pin the ground plan to your drawing board.

THE SCALE MODEL

Always treat the model as a rough. If you lavish too much care and detail on it, you will be depressed or furious (according to your nature) when you find that the director does not like it and wants so many modifications that you have to do it all again. Leave out any detail from the first model. You will be less inhibited about improving it later and allow yourself more leeway for change. Also it is much quicker.

The simplest form of model, which suits ballet or revue, is obviously an arrangement of flat painted planes: cloths, wings and borders can be cut to scale out of heavy paper or card, painted and set up like a Penny Plain, Twopence Coloured Toy Theatre. You may have to make a wooden frame to hang the pieces on, but they will be easily read by the scene painter. Unless you know how to reproduce the effect, do not use water-colour, chalk, pastel or oil colour; this would drive the average scene painter mad (possibly with delight, but it's expensive delight). Use poster colours, designers' colours, gouache or tempera colours – all of which can be easily matched in scene paint (see section 6).

A conventional box set, with the walls all adjoining, is easily made to scale out of white cardboard scored lightly with a knife where angles are required – on the inside to bend outwards, on the outside to bend inwards. It is easiest to measure and cut windows and doors and to paint and let the card dry before folding the walls. Leave half an inch or a centimetre below the bottom of the card, scored horizontally, so that you can stick or thumb-tack the card to the base where you have drawn out the ground plan (see fig 18).

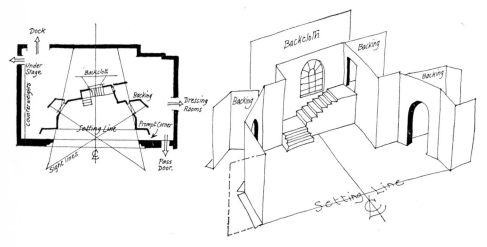

FIG 18   Ground plan and cardboard model of conventional box set

These are obviously only basic instructions which you will have to adapt in practice. You may have designed a set that does not have a straight run of walls, and need to add alcoves, staircases, pillars, rostrums, etc. Alcoves and recesses are an extension of the same principle of folded card; staircases can be made by scoring card on the edge of the rise and treads, but I find using wood is quicker. Pillars can be made of rolled paper, but wooden dowel can be cheaply bought in many diameters. Rostrums again can be made of folded card, but wood is quicker.

To progress from the box set to an open set is like letting in the fresh air. You imagine an open space, and the boundaries are yours. It is a space in which anything can happen. You can surround it with black velvet curtains or a cyclorama of any colour, or simply leave the back and side walls of the hall or theatre as they are. For the action of the play you may need some structure: a mansion perhaps; a pageant cart or a trestle stage; maybe a sloping rostrum with three doors upstage, or just a flight of crooked stairs with a door at the top. Whatever you plan, you will have to make a model to show to the director and afterwards to the actors. Never forget how important it is for the actors to have an idea of the atmosphere of the setting before they start work on the play; and for this reason, be ready with the designs before the first reading.

Balsa wood is by far the easiest medium in which to work the model for a constructed setting. You can buy it economically in many shops – particularly those catering for model aircraft enthusiasts. Balsa is easy to cut, with a sharp knife along the grain and with a fine saw across the grain. It is so soft that you must take care while sandpapering – the swiftest rub with the finest glasspaper will lose you inches in scale. Therefore always cut slightly larger than you need. Being soft, it is very absorbent; so if you want to paint it, allow for the colour seeping in and going a bit flat. It is as well to give a priming coat if you want a strong bright colour or small detail. For glueing, any of the synthetic resin bonds will serve to join balsa to card, or to itself. I have found clear Bostic (Elmer's glue) the most useful.

Metal and wire are rather intractable on a small scale for a model, but can be used if they are the only way of expressing the idea. Cooking foil (glazed or plain silver) for metallic surfaces, and plaster or modeling paste for building up texture on flat surfaces, can be used, but these are all really a waste of time on a model. The actual material that is to be used should be implied and not given. The energy of the designer should not be wasted on producing a beautiful model, but on indicating the appropriate atmosphere for the play in the form of a three-dimensional sketch.

It is very important at the model-making stage that the designer has a clear idea of how the set is going to be lit. I will go into this in more detail later, but for the moment consider that there are two essentials where lighting is concerned: (1) the actors must be seen, (2) the setting must evoke the right atmosphere. *The first of these precepts always takes precedence over the second.* Design your setting, therefore, so that the necessary lighting of the actors does not destroy some subtle, beautiful and useless effect of paint or texture that you are playing around with. The actor comes first; he carries the burden of the play, you don't. Your job is to make the burden lighter and to contribute to the whole.

Finish the model and show it to the director. If he doesn't like it, you must explain carefully to him why he *should* like it, because by now you can justify both emotionally and mechanically everything that you have sensed, appraised, and achieved in the model. In your imagination you have already built and lit the set, and there are the actors walking about in it. The thing's done and yet he doesn't like it.

You must look at it now from the director's point of view. That door is too narrow for the trunk that has to be carried in in act two – which you had forgotten or suppressed in your excitement about the texture of the wall on that side. Those stairs are *far* too steep, not only to carry up that trunk (which you forgot) but for Evelina to come *down* in her ballroom dress in act three. The director being a man of great common sense, and we hope tact, prevails. So you will have to adjust or remake the model. If you had really understood each other to start with this need never have happened. But there it is.

Let us assume now that the model has passed scrutiny and that only slight modifications have to be made. Your next exercise is to make working drawings for the carpenter – even if you are the carpenter yourself. This means making elevations of everything in the plan, and large scale drawings of details and of odd pieces such as rocks or trees. For details, a happy scale is one and a half inches to the foot (1 : 8); or an even larger scale for smaller detail, such as hand props, at three inches to the foot (1 : 4).

If this is a big production, with a lot of scenery, you would be well advised to do your working drawings on good quality tracing paper – with not too soft a pencil – and to have blue prints or dyelines made of them. These cost little and are quickly done 'while you wait' by printers who specialize in this work in almost every town. Drawings are easily lost, and it is a sensible safeguard to have copies to hand out.

Anything that cannot be hired, borrowed or acquired by other means must be designed and made. Sometimes it is cheaper to make than to hire furniture. It is never worth the labour of making more than token suggestions of furniture for a model unless you have all the time in the world – and you never will have. But you must develop a deal of sensitivity to furniture – to its history and to the way it is being made now and is going to be made in the future. You must certainly be able to design chairs and tables that can be sat on or eaten off in any known period of history. One day you may be called upon to do a play without scenery; and then you will see how important furniture is.

Other properties can range from dragons to dustbins; and the craft of prop-making really requires another book. But common sense, ingenuity and imagination can usually provide what is required. Hand props, carried or worn by the actors, are generally considered to be in the precinct of the costume designer.

The next stage is to complete all the working drawings and go over them with the carpenter in great detail in order to make absolutely sure that your designs are crystal clear and capable of being built. If he is a good carpenter he will almost certainly suggest simplifications which you had never thought of, for that is his job. Gradually you will learn how to cut your designs down to the essential, and the more you know about construction the more the carpenter will bless you. But that is for the next chapter.

5 Building

Stage scenery is conventionally made of wood and canvas, and consists of flats and rostrums. Flats are wooden frames over which canvas is stretched and painted. Rostrums are blocks for raising the level of a part of the stage. Small rostrums are usually built solid, but larger ones have removable tops of floorboard or blockboard, which rest on a folding frame.

There are four basic joints used in all woodwork (see fig 19):

FIG 19
Wood joints:

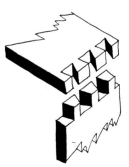

Dove Tail

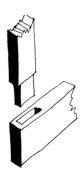

Rabbet

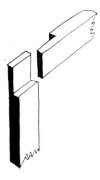

Half-check

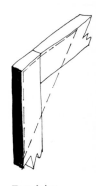

Butt joint

THE DOVE TAIL This is rarely used in the theatre, as it takes rather a long time to cut and fit, but it is the best joint for the sides of a small solid rostrum, 6–9 in. high, which has to last.

THE RABBET OR REBATE This is also called the MORTISE AND TENON joint, and consists of making a slot in one piece of wood, fitting another piece of wood to suit it, then pegging them together. Big carpenter's shops usually have a mortise machine, but you will probably have to drill your mortise with a brace and bit, and clean out with a mortise chisel. This will produce a hidden mortise, such as is used for furniture making. An *open mortise* is simpler to cut.

THE HALF-CHECK OR HALVING is an easier joint to make but not so strong.

THE BUTT JOINT is the simplest; it is made by placing two pieces of wood at right-angles and then glueing and screwing a triangular plate of plywood over.

The standard size of 3 × 1 in. planed deal is used for all framework. The frame of a flat consists of two vertical members called stiles, and horizontal members called rails. The height of the flat depends of course on your design, but many theatres in fact have a standard size for plain flats suitable for the stage. All repertory theatres have stocks of flats which are repainted and used over and over again. When the paint gets too thick they have to be scrubbed down or recanvassed. A well-made flat can last a long time.

For a flat 10 or 12 ft high, only three rails are needed. The top and bottom rails must be the full width of the flat to protect the end grain of the stile, which might otherwise catch on something and split. A hidden mortise in the bottom rail is wise, for this reason. The centre rail is called the toggle rail, because it is mortised into two toggles or shoes which are then screwed on to the inside of the stiles – you must never weaken the stile by cutting into it. Properly the toggle rail should be of slightly thinner wood, so that it does not touch the canvas and show a line across the flat when you are painting. The function of the toggle rail, apart from general strengthening, is to prevent the stiles from bending inward under the tension caused by the paint drying out. You will need two toggle rails on any flat higher than 14 ft. It is customary to put braces across two corners of the flat. Strictly the tenons should be pegged, and not glued, into the mortise, so that flats can be adapted with the minimum wastage (see fig 20).

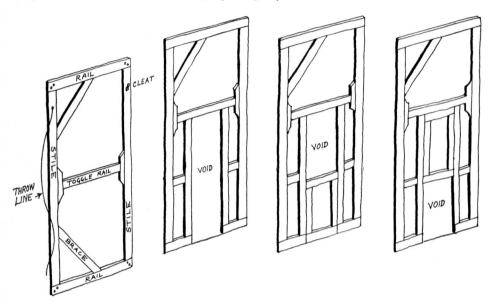

FIG 20   Construction of a plain flat, with variations for door, window and fireplace

The width of the flat is again governed by your design, but it is as well not to go wider than 6 ft 6 in. or 7 ft for reasons of transport. One has heard stories of flats that had to be remade because they couldn't get out of the carpenter's shop door. If you want to go wider than 7 ft it is as well to hinge two flats together and canvas over both, to make two-fold or booked flats, which can either be used in a straight line, or folded inwards to an angle.

Good quality scenic canvas, made of flax or cotton duck, can be bought ready fireproofed, usually 72 in. wide. Hessian is much cheaper but not so long-lived. When I was designing *Back to Methuselah* at the Arts Theatre in London soon after the war, I was lucky enough to find 12 ft wide sailcloth, which we used for a cyclorama – with only two horizontal seams. These large widths are easier to get now, though 72 in. is wide enough for flats.

Cut your canvas slightly more than the width of the flat, and tack it along the top rail, placing your tacks at least two inches in from the outer edge. Now tack along the bottom rail, straining the canvas as you tack, to avoid wrinkles. Then tack the canvas to the stiles, keeping a good tension all the time.

Now your glue pot should be boiling. Fold back the canvas from the outer edge and brush the glue on to the frame. Press down the canvas with a damp rag, smoothing it as you go. The final step is to trim the surplus canvas with a very sharp trimming knife, an eighth to a half inch in from the outer edge. The action of the knife will bury the edge of the canvas into the frame.

When the glue is dry, the flat will be ready for priming and painting – which will be discussed later. Meanwhile how does the frame stand up when it is finished? There are four possible methods:

1 A throwline or lashline of sash cord is attached to the back of the left-hand stile about 1 ft from the top. This line, which is a few inches shorter than the length of the flat, is flicked over a cleat placed at the same height on the back of the right-hand stile of the next flat.

   The line is then pulled tight and passed round a screw or a cleat on the original flat, about 3 ft from the floor; it then goes round a corresponding screw or cleat on the next flat, and is tied off. This action takes a couple of seconds to accomplish and 'striking' is even quicker. In making a series of flats or building up stock, try to standardize the positions of the cleats, so that when flats are re-used in another show in different positions the lines and cleats will always match.

2 A flat standing on its own is supported by a stage brace – an iron rod with a hook at the top, which is passed through a screw-eye in the back of the flat. The brace has an angled foot which is held down by a stage weight or stage screw. The modern form of stage brace is extendable, on the telescopic principle, with a wing nut to fix it at the required length (see fig 21).

3 Another form of support is the french brace or jack, which works on the same principle. This is a triangular frame of 3 × 1 in. timber hinged to the back of the flat. Stage weights, whether round, square or rectangular, are always made with a slot to accommodate the foot of any brace.

4 The final form of support is flying. Two ropes from the grid are passed through screw-eyes on the top rail of the flat and tied off on hanging irons screwed to the bottom rail. Wire is often used in the same way. Sometimes a snap hook is used to fasten the rope or wire to the hanging iron, if the rope or wire is to 'go out' after the piece is in position. This is known as a grummet line. When it is unclipped from the flat, a sandbag must be attached to the line, to compensate for loss of weight.

When several flats are to be flown together – for example, as the back wall of a scene – they are laid face down on the stage floor, battened together with lengths of 3 × 1 in. wood, and flown as described above. The combination is known as a French flat.

So far we have only discussed plain flats that are completely covered with canvas. There are many other varieties: door flats, window flats, archways, fireplaces. These are all made on the same system, but with an inner frame left empty to receive the door, window or fireplace. A door flat can be easily converted into a window or fireplace, by filling in the lower or upper half of the opening.

SCREW EYE IN STILE OF FLAT

WING NUT

STAGE WEIGHT

FIG 21   Extending stage brace

The simplest form of door flat is made by hingeing the door directly to the flat. This, however, is not recommended; it may be cheap but it looks cheap too, as the canvas always flaps when the door is opened or shut. It is far more satisfactory to make a door with a frame of its own that will fit into the opening in the flat. The result will be much more solid, and can be separately braced. The same goes for windows, and for the thickness or reveal of an arch, which can be cleated or 'buttoned' to the back of the flat with a wooden catch or a strap hinge.

Flats that require a shaped edge are called profile flats. Fireproofed plywood is attached to the edge of the flat before it is canvassed, and then cut to the appropriate silhouette. A ground row is a flat on its side, similarly profiled and painted to represent the middle or far distance.

A cutout is an irregular flat, covered with plywood before being canvassed. The stiles and rails must be placed so that they do not come where you need to cut. A simple example of this technique is a cutout ground row of a balustrade – where obviously it is easy to place your toggle rails where they will not interfere with the design. More complicated is a tree flat, which has to be drawn out very carefully; in fact the placing of the stiles dominates the design (see fig 22).

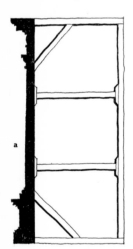 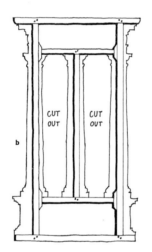 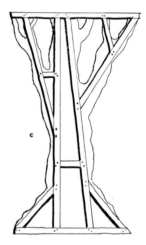

FIG 22a A profile of plywood fixed to the face of the flat before canvassing.
    b Modified stiles and rails to suit cutout.   c Irregular cutout

The only other flat-built pieces that need concern us are backings, which are either single flats braced, or small freestanding booked flats to 'mask' outside a door or window. Rostrum fronts, and the sides of a staircase with, perhaps, a handrail attached are usually built on the principle of the framed flat. Ceiling pieces are usually made booked – opened out, battened and flown on two sets of lines; one set being supplied with snaphooks, which are unclipped when the ceiling is flown out vertically for storage.

CLOTHS OR DROPS

These are made from lengths of canvas sewn horizontally and fixed at the top and bottom to lengths of wooden batten on both sides – known as sandwich battens. The purpose of these battens is (a) to keep them hanging flat, (b) to facilitate rolling the cloth for transport or storage. The functions of the front cloth and back cloth are obvious. In addition you may want to use a cut cloth or cutout drop, for which you may have to attach gauze for strengthening; this will be discussed later.

Finally there is the stage cloth or ground cloth which is stretched over the stage floor and painted with paving, marble, cobblestones, mosaic, floorboards or whatever you wish.

SOLID PIECES

We now leave flat scenery for the moment and concentrate on pieces that have to be solid – pieces which are going to be walked up, trodden or sat upon in the action of the play. This does not include pieces to which a solid texture is to be given; they will be dealt with later.

Platforms in England are called rostrums (they should be rostra, but we are not purists in the theatre); in America they are known as parallels.

The simplest form of rostrum is a single step, made solid, as mentioned at the beginning of this chapter. Floor board or block board is nailed or screwed to timbers set on edge, which have been dovetailed or butted together with strengthening inside. The result is a large shallow box with the underside open which can not only be used on the floor as one step, but can also be 'legged up' higher by bolting 2×4 in. members to the four corners. In addition, it can be bolted between two higher rostrums, to make a bridge (see fig 23).

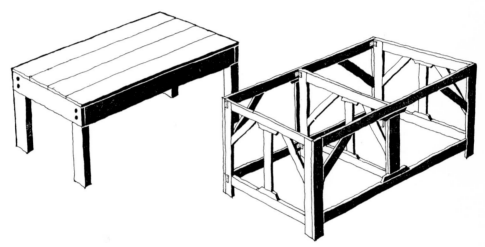

FIG 23   Simple solid rostrum 'legged up', and folding rostrum frame with three hingeing gates

All rostrum tops should be covered with felt and canvas, the canvas being nailed and glued on the same principle as the canvas covering of a flat. On solid rostrums, like those described above, it is usual to carry the canvas down over the sides and to nail and glue underneath.

The folding rostrum (see fig 23) is made of a series of frames, known as gates, hinged together. The top is detachable for packing – again made of floor board or block board, with battening or blocks on the underside to fit into the frame of the structure below. Hingeing is usually carried out in one of two ways. Either it is done in the form of a parallelogram – when folded, the total length is the addition of the length to the width – which means that all the gates are hinged to open and close in the same direction; or the end gates are divided into two halves that fold inwards like two small booked flats, with the result that any supporting gates in the middle of the frame cannot be hinged, but must be set in slots and removed before the frame is closed. The latter 'concertina' method means that the frames when stored do not take up more space than their own length.

When working in a theatre which has a certain amount of stock scenery and a continuity of policy, it is always best to design with stock sizes in mind – and to add extra pieces when required which can be broken up afterwards, leaving the stock unit intact.

Three feet square, 3 × 6 ft and 3 × 9 ft are obviously useful standard rostrum tops. The metric equivalent would be 1 × 1 metre, 1 × 2 metres or 1 × 3 metres.

The height of the framework is a matter of choice, governed at its maximum only by the vertical sight lines of the theatre. It is no use building a 10 ft rostrum in a theatre where the back of the audience cannot see above an actor's navel when he arrives there.

Make your units, say, 1 ft, 2 ft, 4 ft and 6 ft – they can always be legged up 6 in. or 1 ft with safety, on the same principle as the solid rostrums described above.

STEPS AND STAIRS

A short run of steps which will probably be used over and over again can be built solidly to advantage: say 3 × 3 ft or a metre square, with three 6 in. rises and 1 ft treads, padded on the treads and canvassed all over. This is the most useful unit size, as it can butt up to a 2 ft rostrum; and placed on a 2 ft rostrum it can butt up to a 4 ft one, etc. Wide steps are often needed, but three treads built solid, 6 ft long, are rather heavy to handle and need at least two extra supports underneath (see fig 24). It is better to make a 3 × 6 ft shape with only two treads, the lower 1 ft and the upper 2 ft, to butt up to a 1 ft rostrum. Add a single 6 × 1 ft × 6 in. on top if you wish to butt up to a 2 ft rostrum. The single step, 6 ft long and 6 in. high, can of course be used with a 1 ft rostrum alone. I have referred throughout to steps being 6 in. rise and 12 in. tread. This is comfortable, and also serviceable for unit purposes. But it may be necessary for an actor to go quickly up a flight of stairs when 6 × 12 in. would take up too much room. Remember that it is easier to go up than to come down, and there may be a girl in a long dress, or a short-sighted actor unable to afford contact lenses, who *has* to come down; and perhaps the theatre isn't covered by insurance for a broken arm. So be careful when you make a steep rise – unless of course it is supposed to lead to an attic or stable loft. A rough rule-of-thumb about step gradients is that a comfortable rise and the tread should multiply to about 72:

> Thus 4 in. × 18 in. – very grand
> 5 in. × 14 in. – grand
> 6 in. × 12 in. – comfortable
> 7 in. × 10 in. – normal
> 8 in. × 9 in. – steep
> 9 in. × 8 in. – very steep

The last two are nearly impossible to come down without a hand rail.

Flights of more than three or four steps are best made on a 'string' (the carpenter's word for the timber that supports the step treads) with a flat iron piece countersunk into the top tread. This has a right-angle bend which drops into a slot in the edge of the rostrum top. The string pieces can either be cut zigzag with rises and treads screwed on to the edges, or left as a plank with treads mortised into the string of 1½ in. or 2 in. timber. If risers are required, the treads should overlap an inch so that the risers can be nailed from top and bottom.

Exits and entrances may have to be made off stage from rostrums, and the string stairway with a wooden rail is the best method for this. If you are very pressed for wing space, a ladder will have to be used behind scenes.

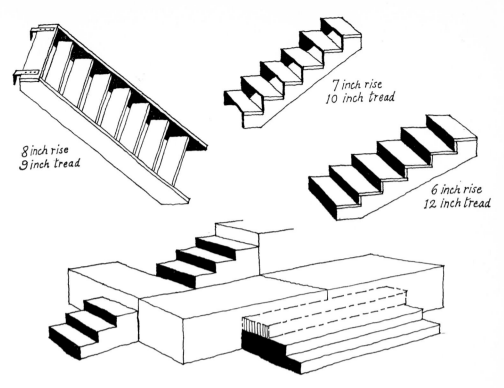

FIG 24   Step units butting up to rostrums as described

OTHER BUILT PIECES

So much for the stock in trade that the amateur and young professional must know about the ordinary pieces required almost all the time in a repertory, club, society or group that puts on plays regularly and intends to go on doing so. But the idea of the permanent unit that will fulfill all needs is highly deceptive. The whole of Piccadilly Circus and Times Square would not provide enough space to store all the *possible* units that you might want.

This is why I said you should keep at the back of your mind, when designing, the stock of the theatre that is paying you for the job. Don't insist on a new 7 ft rostrum when you can do with a 6 ft one adapted. If you are engaged by a repertory or stock company, find out immediately from the carpenter or stage manager the sizes of every piece in stock and note them down. If necessary, make token models of them to scale and design your sets with them. Your ingenuity may be taxed, but you won't lose your job. The very limitation of the field will create a situation to which your imagination will have to respond. Amateur companies likewise build up stocks over the years, or draw on the stocks of a local theatre; and the same point therefore applies.

Nevertheless there is bound to come a time when you have to make a piece that you cannot find in stock, or for a manager who wants the production built from scratch. If you wish to go berserk and spend all his money, you will probably do so whether you read this chapter or not, and it is bad luck on him. But if you have learnt your craft properly, there are a hundred ways in which you can save money and time – not only in construction, but in transport and handling by the stage crew – without curbing your inspiration for a split second. This is not altruism but common sense – and why should a designer not have common sense? Vision and imagination are useless alone, without the common sense to fulfill the imagination and realize the vision.

The 'rake' or 'ramp' is a sloping rostrum – wedge-shaped in section, rising from the stage floor to meet a desirable rostrum. A whole stage may be raked. In the old days a 'full rake' was one inch to the foot, a 'half rake', half an inch to the foot. It never bothered the scenic architects very much; they either compensated for it or, later, ignored it. Nowadays most stages are built as flat as a spirit level can make them, so that if you want a raked stage you must build it on top. This is costly; but a small low ramp is simply a variation of the solid built rostrum and is another of the units that would help to fill up Piccadilly or Times Square. 3 × 6 ft starting from o in. and going up to +12 in. is a nice gentle slope of 1 in 6. Actors will have no difficulty in walking up or down this. But double it to 1 in 3, or o in. to 24 in., and you will get complaints. All these facts have to be known, assimilated, understood and drawn on when the moment calls for them.

Pillars that have to be solid are usually made three-quarters round, with skin ply (fire proofed) nailed at intervals to round 'formers' (sections of timber cut to form the shape within the ply). These are connected together by a central shaft of say

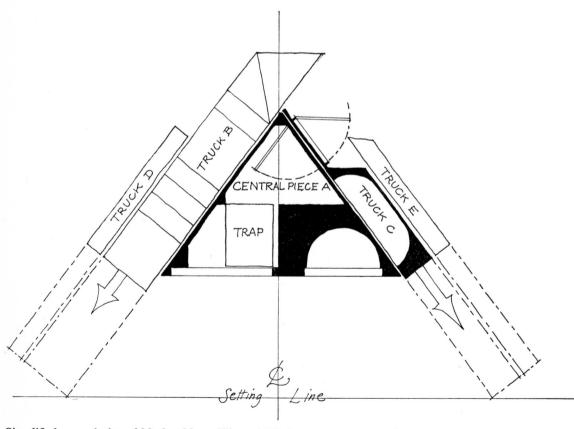

Simplified ground plan of Motley *Merry Wives of Windsor*, Stratford upon Avon, 1955, showing astute planning of trucks. See plates opposite

64

30/31/32

MOTLEY: *The Merry Wives of Windsor.*
Three scenes for The Royal Shakespeare Theatre, Stratford upon Avon 1955.
Photos: Peter Streuli (*See plan opposite.*)

33 JOCELYN HERBERT: *Serjeant Musgrave's Dance* by John Arden. Royal Court Theatre, London 1959

34 MICHAEL WARRE: *Richard II*. Old Vic Company, New Theatre, London 1947

35 NICHOLAS GEORGIADIS: *Electra* by Jean Giraudoux. Oxford Playhouse, 1956.
Reproduced by permission of David Hepburn and Peter Wright

36 MING CHO LEE: *Antony and Cleopatra*. Model for New York Shakespeare Festival, 1963.
Photo: Bill Pierce

37 ANTONIO LOPEZ MANCERA: *Life is a Dream* by Calderón de la Barca.
Teatro Fabregas, Mexico 1964

38 MOLLY MACEWEN: *The Three Estates* by Sir David Lindsay for Sir Tyrone Guthrie's
open stage production, Assembly Hall, Edinburgh 1948.
Photo: The Scotsman

39 HANS VAN NORDEN: *The Spaniard of Brabant* by Gerbrand Bredero. Rotterdam 1961.
Photo: Lemaire en Wennink

40 TANYA MOISEIWITSCH: *All's Well That Ends Well*, for Sir Tyrone Guthrie's open stage
production, Stratford Shakespeare Festival, Ontario 1953.
Photo: Peter Smith

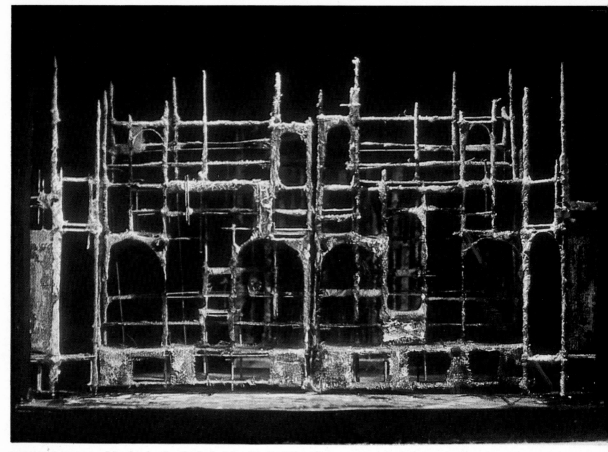

41 RALPH KOLTAI: *Murder in the Cathedral* by T. S. Eliot and Pizetti. Model for Sadler's Wells Opera House, London 1962.

42/43
RALPH KOLTAI: *Don Giovanni* by Lorenzo da Ponte and Wolfgang Amadeus Mozart. Models for The Scottish Opera Company, 1964

44   YOLANDE SONNABEND: *Khovanshtchina* by Modest Petrovitch Moussorgsky.
Project for Royal Opera House, Covent Garden, London 1964

45   EDWARD A. CRAIG: *Macbeth*. Royal Shakespeare Theatre, Stratford upon Avon 1950

46/47
MICHAEL WARRE: *Hamlet*. Models for Alec Clunes. Arts Theatre, London 1945
(*See plan opposite*)

$1\frac{1}{2}$ in. square which travels the whole length of the shaft, slotting into the base and into the architrave. The ply is usually canvassed for painting.

Rocks, trees and banks are comparatively simple to indicate, but need a lot of practice to make convincing if you are seeking naturalism. The conventional method is to make an irregular wooden framework and then to fasten on to it oblique or rounded surfaces of fine-meshed chicken wire, upon which fire-proofed felt and canvas are glued and tacked. The painting afterwards is naturally very important, but more important still is that you make absolutely firm and solid any part of a built piece that is likely to be trodden or sat upon or leaned against; nothing is worse than a nasty crackle of sized canvas yielding to sudden pressure. Make your built pieces intelligently – which means design them well – and you will have no complaints (see fig 25).

We have mentioned trees, rocks and banks, but there are other built pieces, such as machinery, aeroplanes, spaceships – all of which require the designer to do some research and to synthesize. What you are able to do depends not so much on your budget as on your imagination – what use you can make of the resources at your command. There is much that cannot be written or taught; but an understanding of materials, and what stresses and strains they can bear, goes a very long way.

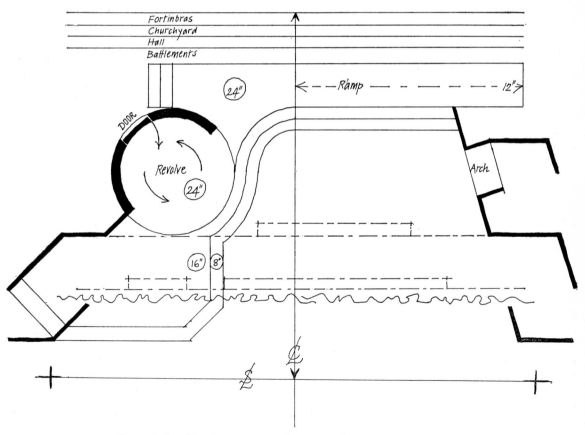

Ground plan *Hamlet*, 1945, see plates opposite

FIG 25 Rock development

BUILDING WITH METAL

Wood will do almost anything you ask it to do in the way of framework if you understand it. Metal can do more, because it can be bent or welded to any shape and still retain its strength. But specially-made metal pieces can be very expensive indeed. Standard lengths of tubular scaffolding are continually used in film studios instead of wooden rostrums. Angled alloy steel and metal, looking like pieces of giant-sized Meccano, are used all the time for exhibition stands and shop displays: Dexion and Apton are two well-known brands. The theatre has been slow to use these. A rostrum supported by metal can be set up and clamped or bolted in half the time it takes to make its wooden counterpart.

Such new possibilities should be investigated. Cost, of course, militates against them; the material is often expensive and needs skill to assemble so that it is safe. But once made, a piece can be used over and over again in different ways, and metal has an advantage over wood in that it takes up less storage space when not being used.

Tubular scaffolding, in particular, needs expert skill to assemble; but marvellous results can be achieved – especially where a wide span or bridge is necessary that would demand impossibly heavy joists if made of wood. Among other designers, John Bury has made some fine sets with the help of tubular construction (see plates 51 and 52).

SURFACE AND TEXTURE

The old way of making a flat surface rough was to glue powdered cork or sawdust on to the canvas. Now there are many plastic materials available that are crying out for use in the theatre – to the designer with a generous budget and time to experiment.

Polystyrene is a dry white foam plastic, as light as a feather, which will absorb scene paint and can be cut clean with a fine-toothed saw or, even better, with a heated knife. There is also a group of synthetic rubbers with which it is well worth experimenting: some of them can be sprayed, some layed on with a trowel; some have first to be moulded and then glued to the surface which requires treatment. Fibreglass is perhaps the most versatile plastic medium. Only personal experiment will reveal the worth of all these new materials to the designer.

SCENE CHANGING METHODS

We have discussed the construction of scenery in a fair amount of detail. A little more must be said about the planning of a whole production as opposed to individual pieces. A play with forty-two scenes, like *Antony and Cleopatra*, obviously does not require forty-two different settings. A revue with thirty numbers is more likely to have variations on a basic theme than thirty separate statements. Where naturalism is not required – as in the two examples above – the problem has been solved to a certain extent by the permanent or semi-permanent set. On the other hand, a naturalistic modern play may have scenes of different locality which must be changed as quickly as possible. There are various means of doing this.

THE REVOLVING STAGE

Apart from its obvious spectacular value, a revolving stage can be very useful for simplifying scene changes. It is quite possible to get two box sets on a revolve of 30 ft diameter. A smaller set can also be set within the upstage room, while the downstage room is in use, and then brought round on cue. This is called an 'inset'; it is frequently used in ordinary practice without any revolve, but a revolve obviously makes it even more practical. One of the difficulties of planning sets on a revolve is to allow sufficient room not only for backings themselves, but for adequate lighting of backings – particularly windows. The plan has to be very carefully conceived in three dimensions. A revolve can also be used in conjunction with the flies. An example of this would be to set only rostrums, carpets and furniture on the revolve, and to 'fly in' back walls or curtains once the revolve is in position.

Some theatres have a built-in revolve, flush with the stage floor, as part of the permanent equipment. It is usually operated electrically from the prompt corner. If a temporary or touring revolve is to be used, circular tracks have to be laid on the stage, segmented rostrums bolted together and wheels fitted to suit the tracks. Curved rostrums are put round the perimeter to make up the stage level.

A small revolve within a semi-permanent setting can be very useful: see design for *Hamlet* (plates 46 and 47 and fig page 73). It is as well to note that a rostrum does not have to round in order to revolve; it can be any shape.

TRUCKS AND WAGGON STAGES

Another mechanical method of changing scenery is the use of trucks or waggons. In its simplest form, a truck is a rostrum on wheels, bearing whatever furniture or scenery is required. This can either be rolled on from the wings during a scene change, or form part of a semi-permanent set which moves during the action into a new position; see the ingenious design by Motley for *The Merry Wives of Windsor* (plates 30–32 and fig page 64).

The size of the truck is governed by the amount of space available in the wings or upstage of the set. Rostrums can be bolted together *ad lib.*, provided they are adequately supported on wheels. In fact half the acting area, or even all of it, can be trucked if there is enough wing space. When this system is built in as a permanent installation it is known as a rolling stage.

LIFTS, TRAPS AND TRICKS

Where lifts or elevators are available, scenery can be set below the stage and brought up to the surface on cue. Formerly worked by a winch or counterweighted hoist (on the same principle as a sash window), lifts are nowadays operated by electrical or hydraulic means.

It is possible for the whole stage area to be built as a lift, either in sections or in one piece, so that a complete setting can be prepared below stage and then raised into position while the upper setting is struck and reset. This is of course very expensive equipment indeed and only likely to be found in large subsidized opera houses.

The traditional English traps of the nineteenth century are still to be found in some theatres. The 'grave trap', about 6 ft by 2 ft 6 in., usually runs across the centre about 7 ft up from the setting line. At the same level, or slightly downstage, are often found two traps about 30 in. square – one each side of the stage. In pantomime these are still sometimes put to their original use – which was to provide a sudden trick entrance through a 'star trap'. The actor, probably the Demon King, would stand on the hoist below the stage while enough load was placed on the counterweight to propel him rapidly up through the floor on cue. The trap was made of hinged triangular flaps which were opened by the velocity of the actor and then fell back into position before he landed. A puff of smoke would conceal the action of the trap. Similar to this was the 'bristle trap', which was made of brush painted to match the floor.

The 'vamp trap', called after Planché's melodrama *The Vampire*, produced in 1820, was a vertical trap door in a flat. By this means the actor would seem to disappear through a solid wall. It consisted of two sprung leaves, painted to match the flat, which automatically closed when the actor was through.

Another useful trick was the 'falling flap'. For a rapid transformation, the top half of a flat would be given a double-sided frame which was hinged across the middle of the flat and painted in with the lower half. On cue, the flap was released, and would drop over the lower half revealing the top of the flat painted in with the reverse of the flap. The Victorians developed this technique to a high art, with many variations and combinations of vertical and horizontal hinged flaps – thus making it possible to transform the scene at a touch of Harlequin's wand. For anyone who will take the care to study it, this kind of magic is still potent. Apart from magical considerations, on a small stage where space is at a premium, this technique can be enormously useful for legitimate scene changes.

6 Painting

Powdered water colour mixed with water and size is the conventional medium for painting canvas and canvas-covered scenery. Distemper and emulsion paints can also be used, but they have a fairly limited range of pale colours, which changes from year to year with the fashions of interior decoration. Black and white can always be obtained, and some firms have a range of strong colours which have to be ordered. They are more expensive than scene paint but have the advantage that they are ready mixed and the surface requires no preparation. I have often used black emulsion on canvas and timber for simple units – it marries well with black velvet and is easy to light.

Dye colours are often used on curtains, because they impregnate the canvas, which therefore remains supple when scene paint and size would make it stiff. The disadvantage of dye colours is that they are difficult to paint over because they tend to 'bleed through' scene paint, sometimes even after two coats.

Oil paint is rarely used in the theatre, except on furniture or props or (thinned with turpentine) on wood. It is expensive, takes longer to dry than scene paint, and cannot be over-painted by any other medium. It is occasionally used to stencil a pattern on curtains, but I think its disadvantages far outweigh its advantage – which is durability. I have only used matt oil paint on rostrum tops and glossy oil paint on ground cloths for marbling; but even then it is no use for touring as it cracks, and the cloth cannot be used again. If you want a shiny surface for a deliberate effect, then oil or lacquer paint is the answer – although a good stiff coat of size on top of water paint (when dry) also gives quite a good sheen. Oil paint on a flat will mean the flat will have to be re-canvassed when next used. On new wood, varnishes and stains can be used – as shiny or matt as you wish. Thinners or turpentine will make matt; Terebine will speed the drying process. Knotting, button polish or shellac (different names for glue dissolved in methylated spirit) is the best primer for wood, has the effect of a light stain and brings out the grain. It seals the surface, and finger marks can be wiped off. It is also the best primer for hardboard.

BRUSHES

For priming and 'laying in', a 5 or 6 in. distemper brush is advisable. If you are painting a large cloth on the floor, a household broom is better. I once watched a painter at the Théâtre National in Brussels lay in a large backcloth design of mine for the *Devil's Disciple* in about twenty minutes. He had three wide tins of paint and three brooms, which he swapped over from time to time, flicking and overlapping the colours.

You will need several 2 in. to 4 in. brushes, a couple each of 1 in. and $\frac{1}{2}$ in., and lining brushes and fitches. These last are for fine work. It is a false economy to buy cheap brushes; the hairs drop out and they do not last. It is also a false economy to have too few brushes; you will spend half your time washing them out when you want to change colour, and then washing again when you find you're going back to the first bucket of paint. *Always* wash your brushes when you have finished work, before the paint and size hardens in the bristles. *Never* leave a brush standing in a paint bucket overnight – or in water. Leave them flat on a table if they are dry, or hang them up by the handle if wet. Buy good brushes, treat them well, and they will last for ages.

COLOURS

As you will have designed the set and made sketches and models yourself with poster or designers' colours, it is good to find that you can buy most of the same range in powder colour. Even designers' colours with an aniline dye base can nearly always be matched. Every designer has his own spectrum of colours, which changes from play to play (and from year to year). But here is a basic list of colours to which you can add:

White	Crimson
Black	Indian Red
Lemon yellow	Emerald green
Chrome yellow	Ultramarine
Vermilion	Prussian blue

These are colours that cannot be invented, and from which you can make any colour, from shocking pink to turquoise. The quantities needed are difficult to advise on here, because the areas to be covered can vary so much – apart from the fact that you may want to do the whole set in two colours only.

The metallic paints – gold and silver – can be made in various ways. For a model or costume design, I buy bronze or aluminium powder by the ounce and mix it on a plate with gum arabic. It can be bought in pots, but I like to be able to control the richness. In larger quantities, for scenery, gold and silver powder can be mixed with size, or bought (more expensively) in a bottle. As with dye colour, metallic paints are difficult to paint over; they tend to show through a covering of scene paint.

STUDIO OR PAINT SHOP

Some theatres and most professional studios are fortunate enough to have a paint frame, to which a cloth or a 'run' of flats can be nailed. The frame is hung in such a way that it can be raised or lowered by windlass or motor. The painter stands on the deck, so to speak, with his palette, buckets and heaters, and can move the frame up and down to suit his eye level. This is by far the easiest way to paint, as all the ingredients are close to hand.

Other ways of painting depend on the size of your studio. It *should* be as big as the stage, so that the carpenter can fit up the whole set to the correct ground plan. This means that you can paint flats, cleated and braced in their right positions, from a ladder, mobile tower or rostrum.

If you have not the space to set up the whole scene in position, either arrange the flats round the walls of the studio and work from a ladder or tower as before or, if there is not sufficient headroom, paint horizontally, either on trestles or on the floor. Cloths, drops and ground cloths will have to be painted on the floor anyhow if there is no paint-frame; so the studio must be big enough for your maximum-sized cloth.

If you have not enough space on the floor of your studio to paint a cloth, or a run of flats, you will have to paint them on stage, and the management and director must allow you time to do this. If they do not, there will not be any scenery.

Wherever you work you must have close access to a gas ring or electric plate – preferably two, of whatever power is most available. The first thing to do is to mix a full bucket of size and water. Size is essential for powder colour, because without it the paint will not fix. Size can be bought in granules or as jelly. Use a pound to a gallon of boiling water and stir till any lumps are dissolved. You must always have a size bucket ready. Never paint without one part of size to one part of dissolved colour, or the paint will come off – not only on costumes and stage hands, but from the flat too.

A second bucket to prepare is of whitening, which looks like lumps of chalk and needs to be broken up and soaked in water. This is a basic leaven that will, like size, always be needed; so have it standing by, ready to mix with size or into other colours. You can buy an intense white in powder which is extra strong, but ordinary whitening is much cheaper and will suffice for the moment. Mixed half-and-half with size, whitening makes a conventional priming coat for new flats and rostrums. But I have always preferred to go nearer to a neutral tone with the primer. In other words, if your main final colour is to be warm, prime with whitening, yellow ochre and a touch of Indian red; if cold, prime with whitening and a little ultramarine. Needless to say, the size is more important than the colour.

A third bucket that you need to have standing by is a good strong mixture of black. I have found that black is a most useful colour. It does not get in the way of the costumes, or of the actors, or of the lighting, or of the director; and it can reveal marvellously and subtly the structure of a built set when it is carefully lit. A black cyclorama or black wall can look as blue as daylight if well lit, and when not lit gives an infinity of depth. But this fondness for black may just be a particular fad of mine. When I was working at the Arts Theatre in London, Fanny Taylor, who was then painting there, used to order fourteen pounds of black paint as soon as she heard I was designing the next show – whatever the show was. At the London Academy of Music and Dramatic Art I once asked the Principal, Michael MacOwan, if I could re-paint the back wall (which was pale blue) because it was shabby. He said yes, and I re-painted it black. The resulting depth was astonishing. The black wall is still there, though we have rebuilt the theatre; it now forms one of the side walls of the auditorium.

You now have three buckets: one of *size*, one of *whitening* (unsized) and one of *black* (unsized). The other eight main colours listed can either be kept in paper bags or tins, and used when required, or be mixed into a paste with water and put into boxes or sections along one side of a large wooden palette about the size and height of a kitchen table. When large quantities of a colour are needed for mixing, take them dry from the powder, add boiling water, and stir in an equal quantity of size. When small quantities are needed for finishing, work from the palette, using diluted size as the liquid medium.

MIXING, MATCHING AND SCALING

You are working to your own design; so you will know already that poster and designers' colours are slightly darker when applied than when they are dried out. To match a dried colour exactly is not easy – particularly if you used a large range of colour for your designs and do not remember the quantities.

The same is true of scene paint. To match the colours of your design, mix to a slightly deeper tone than your eye tells you you need. When the mixture is made, dip in a piece of paper or white canvas, dry it out over the heater, and *then* compare it with your original. This may sound maddening but it is well worthwhile, and becomes second nature once you know the trick. It is best to be systematic about it. *Always* dry out a sample, and watch it before painting; you will save yourself hours of irritable repainting if you do. Check all the colours you have used – as designer – and mix and match them before starting to paint – as painter. If you avoid doing so because you are in a great hurry, you could be lucky, but it isn't worth chancing.

You are now almost ready to paint – but not quite. First (as I mentioned earlier) it is necessary to put on a priming coat of a suitable tone, whether on flat, cloth or rostrum. This must be 50 per cent size and 50 per cent colour – or whitening, if you are going to use very light colours or very thin glazed colours.

Once the priming is on the canvas and dry, the problem is how to scale up the $\frac{1}{2}$ in. model to 24 times the size. For a single flat, say 6×12 ft, this is easy; it can be done by eye if it is a free design; or with a ruler if not. But a cloth or drop 24×18 ft presents a special problem. To start with, your eye cannot encompass the whole cloth while one arm is at brush length and the other arm is holding a bit of the model 12×9 in. The practical answer is simple; you must make a grid of, say, $1\frac{1}{2}$ sq. in. on the model, and correspondingly grid the cloth in 3 ft squares. The best way to do this on the model (if you do not mind spoiling it) is to rule squares in pencil on it; if you wish to preserve the model as a work of art, draw squares on a piece of cellophane laid over it. For the cloth, it is necessary to have a long piece of string and either a willing helper or a hammer and nail. Measure and mark the edges of the cloth at 3 ft intervals, and then rub chalk or charcoal along the piece of string. Nail the string at the first mark, stretch it across to the corresponding point, then snap it on to the cloth like a bow string; it will deposit a line of chalk or charcoal. Go along the cloth at 3 ft intervals, then across, and you will have made your grid – one that corresponds to the grid or model but is 24 times larger. Now draw in the shape of the design from square to square in charcoal, chalk or with a brush, and then get on with the painting. The grid will soon be lost or brushed out while you paint.

TEXTURE

Among the many possible painting techniques for simulating texture are the following:

SCUMBLING – 'worrying' the wet paint with the brush, as you put it on, so that the paint is of an uneven texture and the underpaint shows through. It is hard work on the wrist, and for the brush.

SPLASHING – flicking the brush, loaded perhaps with another colour, either while the paint is wet (fairly enthusiastically) or on the stage after the scene is set (with great discretion). At either time, you are liable to get as much paint in your hair as on the canvas. A less primitive way of providing the same effect is spraying.

SPRAYING – which requires the use of a spray gun, the most economic form of which can be inserted in the wrong end of a vacuum cleaner and the tube connected to a jar with a spray attachment. By adjusting the needle in the gun you can get a fine or a coarse spray. When using a broad spray be careful not to let the colour drip by having it too thin. The spray is very useful for stencilling wallpaper or repeating patterns.

STIPPLING – a stipple brush was not included in the list of brushes, because it is almost obsolete – the spray gun having taken its place. But you can stipple with an old brush, using rather dry colour and dabbing on dots of paint with the brush held at right-angles to the canvas.

RAGROLL – an interesting texture can be produced on a flat by rolling a dry rag up or across it before the paint is dry.

LINING – though not strictly texturing, this is a fundamental part of the scene painter's craft and must be described. Skirting boards, chair rails, panelling and cornices or picture rails often have to be indicated in a representational setting. You must get yourself a straight edge or ruler and place it flat down (or up) along the face of the canvas. Take a fitch, liner or $\frac{1}{2}$ in. brush, loaded with your highlight colour, and run it along the straight edge. If you are painting a cornice, or a chair rail or dado, on a run of flats, make sure that you measure the distances from the *bottom* of the flats. When you have finished lining the highlight, wipe the straight edge clean and proceed with the shadow lines on the same principle. Unless you are painting a very wide cornice you will not need a middle tone. Before the paint is entirely dry, take a clean brush and clear water, and run the wet brush dipped in clear water along the painted moulding, overlapping the highlight and the shadow. The dark and the light will blend and provide a middle tone. Don't on any account go over the same place twice or you'll wash the paint off. One clean stroke is enough.

WALLPAPER – again this is not strictly texturing, but in a way it has the same effect. Two methods involve stencilling. With the first, the pattern is completely cut through a heavy stencil paper on thin card. With the second, the pattern is indicated by perforating the stencil with dots tracing the design, which is then 'pounced' on to the canvas with a soft bag full of powdered charcoal.

A third method is to 'grid' the flats (as described above) by 'snapping' a string rubbed with charcoal or chalk at suitable vertical and horizontal intervals, and then to carry out the pattern free hand.

A general note about wallpaper and patterned surfaces: always use a broken ground underneath – even if the paper is to look as fresh as a new pin – particularly when painting with pale colours. It is helpful to the lighting, to the actors and to the concentration of the audience if you grade interior wall flats so that they deepen in tone at the top. If the difference in tone between the top and bottom is fairly marked, it is sometimes effective to swap over the tone of the wallpaper stencil about two-thirds of the way up – dark pattern on light ground below, and reversed above. You may need a neutral tone to make the transition.

BUILT PIECE, CUTOUT PIECE, ETC.

Built pieces will often utilize flat planes in construction which, even if textured with cork, sawdust or plastic as described above, will need paint as well to break the surface. The same of course applies to a cutout piece. The important thing is to determine the general direction of light – so that you can shadow and highlight on the right sides – and avoid re-painting after the production is lit.

If the built pieces are part of an outdoor naturalistic set, they will need keying in with the stage cloth, by the use of a common ground colour and then perhaps spraying or splashing over when set. (This also leaves a silhouette on the ground cloth which helps the stage manager to set the piece.)

Cut cloths can be painted on a paint frame or on the floor. *Always* paint before cutting; wet paint will curl the canvas. Scale up the cloth and mark where you want to cut. If the design consists of pillars, or more or less straight tree trunks, you may get away with glueing another thickness of canvas folded back from the edges – but this will not guarantee that there is no curling. Far the best way is to lay the finished cloth face down, and glue net or gauze across the openings. This is essential where you have a complicated design, containing unsupported horizontal or 'undercut' shapes. If there is to be an entrance through a cut cloth, it must be designed so that the net or gauze supports the shape, but does not get in the way. Another way to achieve this is to use a short cut cloth or deep cut border, and to run-in profiled or cut flats behind.

GAUZES

Gauzes have always been popular in the theatre of illusion, both for transformation scenes, and for creating a misty-distance unreality or the removal of action away from the audience.

The technique of using gauzes depends entirely on lighting. Roughly speaking, when lit from in front a gauze (with whatever is painted on it) appears as solid as a cloth – provided there is no light behind or such light as there is (which may be necessary for a scene change) is cut off by a curtain or dark cloth directly behind the gauze. When the scene change upstage is completed, the curtain or cloth is flown out and the light comes up on the new setting behind the gauze. *Provided all light is taken away from in front*, the gauze will completely disappear and can be flown out virtually unnoticed before front light is brought in again. This is the transformation so beloved by the Victorians.

There are other ways of using gauzes, however: plain, with a little light in front, to give a smoky distance, or to project clouds upon; painted and lit from in front (while the stage is also lit) to give the effect of looking *through* something, whether representational or symbolical; or daubed with thick paint or appliqué, to make a silhouette (again through which the action is seen). Remember, though, that as long as there is light in front or anything solid on the surface, the gauze will always be seen 'going out'.

I mentioned thick paint on purpose, because scene paint and size tends to congeal in the fine mesh of the gauze unless used very thin. This is why transformation gauzes should properly be painted with dye colours – so that the threads of gauze are stained with colour and not clotted with it.

A final word about painting. Always keep some of your main colours for touching up when the scene is set up on the stage.

7 The set up

We have seen that scenery must be built as lightly and as strongly as possible, and that it must be possible to take it out of the studio on to a lorry or a train and into the theatre, without having to be cut up or rebuilt on the way. If the workshop is near the stage, and you are building a standing set for a short run of performances, there is an opportunity to build with scaffolding and experiment with applied surfaces such as plaster and cement which do not travel well; plastic surfaces are more tensile and will travel better.

Once the scenery arrives in the theatre, anything to be flown should be dealt with first. This applies to the lighting above the stage and to any cloths, borders, french flats or built pieces. By now the carpenter will have the 'fly plot' or 'hanging chart', and the 'light plot' will tell the electrician of any lamps, battens, border lights or floods that cannot be hung after the scene is set. All these must be hung now – even if they are not accurately positioned until later.

Any painted cloths or drops are now laid, rolled, and in position ready to be hung. The hanging can be done by two methods. The first is to fasten the top batten of the cloth to ropes that pass through pulleys above the grid into tackle on one side, and thence to the 'fly floor' or stage floor, where they are tied off on a cleat. The ropes are known as 'hemp lines' and have to be man-handled. This system of flying has been used for centuries, with refinements like the 'drum and shaft' and the 'windlass' which reduce the strain on the operator.

Much more efficient – and much more costly to install – is the second, or counter-weighted, system of flying, which is now universally adopted in modern theatres. By this system the cloth is fixed by means of clamps to an iron barrel or pipe, which is suspended by wires from pulleys above the grid; and the wires are carried through sheaves to a cradle holding counterweights. When the cloth is unrolled and raised off the stage floor, sufficient counterweights are loaded into the cradle to balance the weight of the cloth, french flat or built piece that is to be flown. By this means much heavier pieces can be flown than could ever be managed on hemp lines, and the operation is effortless, silent and swift.

When everything you wish to fly is out of the way and hung in its right position from the grid, the stage or ground cloth is unfolded and laid down – much as you would lay a carpet by kicking outwards from the centre, and taking a strain as you tack down the edges. In a conventional theatre the front of the cloth is usually not tacked, but buried in the 'carpet cut' – a long narrow trap which secures the front edge of the cloth.

Next, any built pieces that have had to travel in sections are reunited (bolted or screwed together) and rostrum gates are unfolded and their tops dropped into position. If the play has a single setting, the rostrums can now be put into position, and any flats be set up to them. A certain amount of adjustment is usually necessary, even if the plan is clearly marked out on the ground cloth. If there is no ground cloth, make chalk or paint marks on the floor which correspond to your ground plan – working up from the setting line and out from the centre line. If the play has more than one setting, you should mark out the scenes in different colours, and plastic tape is best for this. Marks for blackout changes can be made in luminous paint – but this is more useful for furniture than for scenery.

Any trucks or waggons must now be assembled and tried out, and revolving pieces tested in their final positions. In short, all the pieces that have been designed, built and painted must now be put into place, seen to work and touched up with paint if they have been rubbed or scratched in transit.

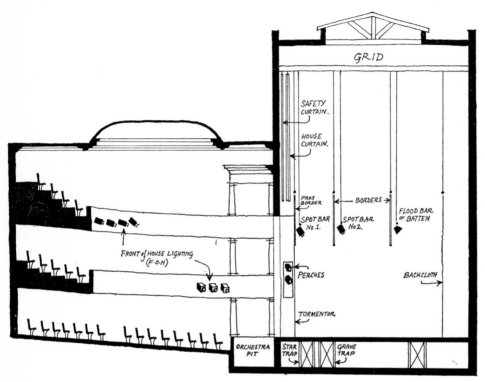

FIG 26   Section of a medium sized nineteenth-century playhouse with modern lighting equipment

STAGE LIGHTING

It is not within the scope of this book to deal with stage lighting in technical detail. It is necessary, however, for the designer to understand the basic principles of current practice. And the more he knows about lighting the better a designer he will be. Paint, contour, volume and texture are the stuff that designers' dreams are made on, but without light they are meaningless. I have never yet directed and designed a production which I have allowed anyone else to light. Lighting is a personal matter much to do with the designer's craft, and must be studied by every aspiring student. Books for further study will be found listed at the end of this volume, but it is necessary to describe briefly here the main types of electric lighting that are used in the theatre at the moment. Focused and selected lighting is of course far more important than general lighting.

GENERAL LIGHTING

The compartment batten or border light is the modern counterpart of the old gas batten. Designed to give a general diffusion of light over a wide angle of coverage, it is admirably suitable for lighting cloths or curtains from above, and the lower part of a cloth or cyclorama from behind a ground row on the stage floor, or from a cut below. When placed in front of the stage above the orchestra pit, it becomes the modern counterpart of the oil floats or gas footlights, offsetting hardlight from above on the actors' faces. Built in a long trough, it houses lamps and reflectors in separate sections wired in three or four circuits, in front of which frames of colour medium can be placed.

The floodlight is a single lamp with a reflector which refracts and diffuses light over a wide area. It is housed in a casing which can be hung from a rail or pipe, or fixed to a stand in the wings. Colour mediums can be slid into a frame in front. The flood can be hooded or masked to contain the spread of light, but this is wasteful.

FOCUSED LIGHTING

Hard-edged or profile spotlights are used to project light in a controlled beam from the front of the house on to the stage, particularly when there is an apron or fore-stage. These spotlights are called hard-edged because they have lenses equipped with an iris, to give a circular beam, and 'barn doors', which are shutters designed to eliminate the spill of light over the auditorium or proscenium. Naturally they can also be used behind the proscenium.

Soft-edged spotlights are designed for use behind the proscenium, or on each side of the apron or forestage from 'boomerangs' or 'perches' arranged vertically. They throw an intense beam, but the soft edge gives a slight diffusion which enables them to overlap and mingle.

Optical projectors work on the principle of the magic lantern. Painted or photographic slides can by this means be thrown on to a backcloth. Cut-out silhouettes can similarly be projected on to the setting or on to the stage floor. The lighting downstage has to be carefully balanced so as not to cast too much reflected light on to the screen.

THE MAKING OF SLIDES

The main difficulty in painting slides is to allow for the distortion that comes from having to project from one side or from above. The simplest geometry, however, will help you to make a grid to save this difficulty. Alternatively you can do your designs square and have them photographed at the exact angle from which they are to be thrown. Transparencies can then be made on glass. Powerful projectors now usually contain an automatic fan, so there is little risk of the slide cracking.

I directed Büchner's *Woyzeck* in London some years ago, and used two 2-kilowatt projectors on the spot bar. One contained a slide of the silhouette of a great knotted tree trunk, the other showed the roof tops of a small German town. They were 'cross faded' on a backcloth which was painted and sprayed with a lot of cloudy texture in different colours, designed to pick up any colour thrown on to it. This proved to have a far more atmospheric effect than a plain white screen would have produced. The only trouble was that the slides cracked under the heat, and I must have repainted them a dozen times before we were done. Modern equipment is much better, and some of the new German projectors have – apart from a cooling fan – complicated iris shutters that will provide not only a full moon of any size, but a half moon and a new moon. Better still for the painter, Reiche and Vogel make projectors that will take slides five and seven inches square. I have myself recently used at LAMDA a new English 2-kilowatt optical projector made by Strand Electric, which I found very easy to handle. Apart from having to allow for distortion, there is another problem in painting a slide: the scale ratio of the paint brush. If you paint a slide – normally $3\frac{1}{4}$ in. square – which is to be projected with a 3 in. lens on to an area 25 ft square at a distance of 20–30 ft, every hair mark of the finest sable will be apparent. Now this may not matter if the rest of your design fits in with it; you need to experiment and decide what kind of definition is required from the projected slide by the design as a whole. If you are aiming to project a severely naturalistic background, you would be best advised to use photography. Photographic slides have the added advantage that copies can be made, and held in reserve for emergencies. If this design is 'free' and you decide to paint it direct on to glass, it is worth knowing that a drop of Acetic Acid washed over the slide and allowed to dry off will give the glass a slight texture, forming an easier ground on which to paint.

In a theatre with a deep stage it is possible to use 'back projection' of film or slides, throwing the image on to the back of a seamless cloth linen drop or plastic screen. Any writing or lettering has of course to be reversed for back projection.

There is undoubtedly a great future in projected scenery – perhaps we shall have stereoscopic projection one day. Meanwhile, no designer should neglect the study of this branch of his craft. It has been used to great effect on the professional stage recently in Joan Littlewood's productions at the Theatre Workshop, Stratford, London; notably in *Oh, What a Lovely War*, where news bulletins, flashed in teletype on to the back of the stage, gave a visual, laconic comment on the scene before or after. Pictorial projection is also used very successfully and frequently in the big German opera houses.

LIGHTING THE PLAY

This can only be a very general note. I have indicated above that the lighting must be planned in broad terms while the production is being designed. At a later stage you will have gone into more detail with the director, the stage manager and the electrician, who may have had to hire special equipment.

By the time the production is set up, all those concerned must know the effect aimed at, the approximate placing of all the lighting equipment and the number of cues for light changes that will have to be plotted once the lamps are positioned. In the simplest possible terms: whatever your equipment, the spotlights should be positioned to give a balanced spread of even light over the acting area. This spread can then be deliberately *unbalanced* by dimming individual spots and by the use of colour mediums.

For the amateur and young professional group playing in small theatres and halls where very little equipment exists it is necessary to carry a portable switchboard and some spotlights. By far the most versatile form of lighting is the soft-edged Fresnel spotlight, which can either be used with an intense narrow beam, or with a wide throw – like a medium-angled floodlight. These today in England can be hired for a pound a week or so, and bought for ten to twenty pounds each according to the power required. They range from 250 to 2,000 watts.

A small portable switchboard with four sliding dimmers controlling eight circuits can be bought for about fifty pounds. A more complicated board with interlocking dimmers costs nearer two hundred pounds.

Fine results can be achieved with very little equipment if used with imagination and foresight. Although the National Theatre switchboard at the Old Vic has 140 circuits, and Covent Garden Opera House 240, often using over 200 spotlights in one opera, it is still quite possible effectively to light a production in a small hall with eight or ten spotlights.

8 Next scene

The designer's job is done when the play is set, lit and in performance. Occasionally minor modifications are necessary later for improving the production. Major alterations which depart from the agreed scheme should be treated compassionately by the designer, as hysterical symptoms which will rapidly disappear at the suggestion of a new contract for redesigning the whole production. Adjustments must be made when things go wrong – but things should not go wrong if the work has been properly prepared and executed, and if the designer has remained in close touch with the director.

INFLUENCE OF FILM AND TELEVISION

Film and television may have taken ideas and talent from the theatre; they have also potentially enriched it. A part of the millions that can now watch the recorded performance of an actor will want to go to see him in the flesh – even if they have never set foot in a theatre before. Broadcasting and recording of music over the last forty years has enormously increased the attendance at concerts. Television and all the fantastic developments of the cinema will end by similarly encouraging the public back into the theatre.

There can never be a substitute for a live production, because it is based on physical contact, and therefore completely undivided; an audience in a theatre can quite unconsciously cause an actor to modify or change his performance entirely. There is another reason, deeper and unacknowledged, but it is fundamental to the enjoyment of theatre. This is the possibility that *something might go wrong*. The actor is a proxy for the fears and hopes of the audience; the ritual of human sacrifice, so clearly expressed in a bull fight, is also buried deep in the theatre.

NEW FORMS OF THEATRE

It is only during the last decade that the interest and concern of theatre people about the buildings where they have to work has begun to be discussed by the layman – a term which must unhappily include the architect. It could well have been the competition of film and television that stimulated the recent interest in open stage and arena theatre at the expense of the proscenium picture frame. If so, this would have represented a box office reaction, based on the idea of making capital out of the one thing film and television cannot do – the presentation of a three-dimensional actor in the midst of an audience. But it is not so, for the impulse towards open stage has come from the small experimental groups, rather than from the big managements; the latter seem content still to fill their picture frames with conventional scenery.

The origin of the renewed interest in the open platform stage in England can be precisely dated – 1881. This was the year that a young actor called William Poel persuaded the president of the New Shakespeare Society to sponsor a production of the first quarto of *Hamlet* on a platform stage in St George's Hall, London. Poel later formed the Elizabethan Stage Society, and up to 1905 had directed some thirty plays on a reconstruction of an Elizabethan platform stage. Harley Granville-Barker, who was mentioned in chapter three, acted *Richard II* for Poel in 1899;

and his subsequent influence on Shakespeare production was largely based on his understanding of the function of the open stage, to which he was introduced by Poel.

Fifty odd years elapsed before the first permanent, modern open stage was built in Stratford, Ontario, at the instigation of Sir Tyrone Guthrie and his designer Tanya Moiseiwitsch. But in the meantime many serious directors, designers and actors had become increasingly frustrated by the conditions in which they were forced to work. Many experiments were made, in England, notably, by Terence Gray at the Cambridge Festival Theatre and by Nugent Monck with his famous amateur company at the Maddermarket Theatre in Norwich. Directors of Shakespeare productions were continually trying to bring the actor forward on an apron stage, but were prevented from coming forward *enough* by the sight-lines of the playhouses.

At the same time the playwrights were trying to break through the fourth-wall convention of the proscenium frame. Luigi Pirandello (1867–1936), the great Italian dramatist, made a mockery of the theatre of illusion by revealing that illusion itself might be an illusion of an illusion. Since Pirandello, there have been many other metaphysical dramatists probing the customs and behaviour of the 'human ant', and writing plays *in spite of* the conditions in which they had to be played.

Martin Esslin has written a comprehensive book called *The Theatre of the Absurd* – a penetrating analysis of such recent dramatists as Beckett, Adamov, Ionesco, Genet and many others. From the designer's point of view these dramatists do not always demand a specific form of presentation. Although what they postulate is unconventional, they sometimes ignore the frame, sometimes accept it. Some of them give specific stage directions, some do not. Among other modern playwrights for the designer to consider are Arrabal, Frisch, Pinget, Pinter and Albee, who should be assessed carefully and calmly – in the horror of your own study. All these are making voluble a deep-seated feeling of anxiety and insecurity which is typical of our age – an age dominated by the shadow of the concentration camp, the atom bomb, racialism, and this must be shown or reflected in designing their plays. It cannot very well be avoided, since the communication is so strong. A door means more than a door, a telephone more than a telephone – yet they are still ordinary doors and ordinary telephones. You must place them so that they become extraordinary doors, and telephones that are full of fear, dread, hatred or love – which must still look normal. This is where the designer faces a metaphysical problem. One answer is to leave out everything that has no bearing on the play – walls included. But this argument of course could apply to the design of any play, and, like all generalizations, is not very helpful. Read the play, and then determine your focal points.

ARENA

Arena staging or theatre-in-the-round is an extreme form of open staging which throws the designer to the lions. There is no wall to put his back to; so he has to make the atmosphere with floor texture – carpets, gravel or parquet – and rostrums, furniture and lighting. This means that he must have a clear idea of the feeling of the play, and be able to communicate it to the audience the moment the lights come up, with the utmost economy and artistry. Doorways represented by battens stuck in stage weights may be all right for rehearsals, but are ludicrous in performance – unless the whole production is treated on that level. Consistency of treatment is also obligatory in the round, and the designer must contrive a consistent scheme.

48/49
PETER BROOK AND DESMOND HEELEY: *Titus Andronicus*. Royal Shakespeare Theatre,
Stratford upon Avon 1955.
Photos: Peter Streuli

50 PETER RICE: *Ariadne auf Naxos* by Hugo von Hofmannsthal and Richard Strauss.
Sadler's Wells Opera House, London 1961

51 JOHN BURY: *The Other Animals* by Ewan MacColl. For Joan Littlewood, Theatre Royal, Stratford East, London 1954. *Photo: J. V. Spinner*

52 JOHN BURY: *You won't always be on top* by Henry Chapman. For Joan Littlewood, Theatre Royal, Stratford East, London 1956. *Photo: J. V. Spinner*

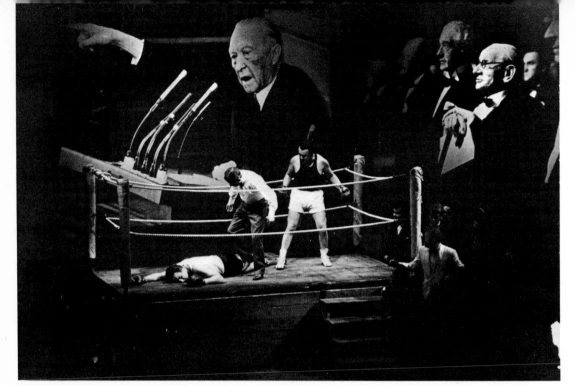

53 RALPH KOLTAI: *The Rise and Fall of the City of Mahagonny* by Bertolt Brecht and Kurt
Weill. Sadler's Wells Opera House, 1963. *Showing the use of projected background*   *Photo: Alexander Low*

54 MING CHO LEE: *Love's Labour's Lost*. New York Shakespeare Festival, 1963.
Photo: Bill Pierce

55 MICHAEL ANNALS: *Jackie the Jumper* by Gwyn Thomas. Royal Court Theatre, 1963.
Reproduced by permission of David Hepburn and Peter Wright

56 ROBERT WINKLER: *Blood Wedding* by Federico Garcia Lorca. Model.
Museum of Contemporary Crafts, New York. Photo: Peter Fink

57 PETER WEXLER: *War and Peace,* adapted from Leo Tolstoy. Model.
Museum of Contemporary Crafts, New York. Photo: Peter Fink

59/60

HENRY BARDON: *Ride a Cock Horse* by David Mercer. Early sketches. Piccadilly Theatre, London 1965

This can be done with carpets and furniture alone, or with the addition of skeleton doorways and window frames, which are less obstructing to the view than might be thought.

In the achievement of successful open stage and arena productions the amateur is often more fortunate than the professional company. The seating arrangements in a flat-floored hall are obviously flexible, where those in a playhouse are not. Figure 27 shows some variants of seating plans in a rectangular hall which are

FIG 27 Various seating arrangements for a flat floored rectangular hall

neither expensive nor complicated to manage. The action of the play can be sited at the end, in the middle, at the side or in a corner of the hall. The ingenuity of the designer may be taxed, but if he and the director know what they are about the most marvellous results can be achieved and atmosphere generated. A small budget demands a large imagination, and this can be seen in a lot of amateur work today.

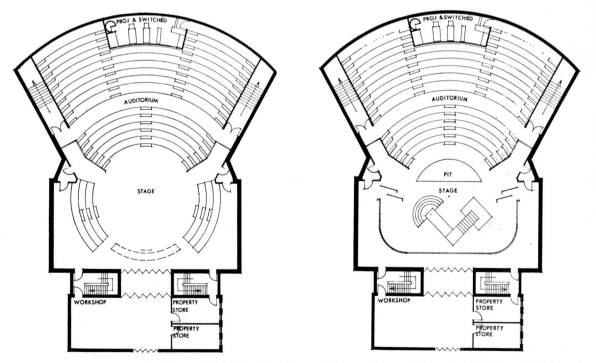

FIG 28 Plans of the Northcote Devon Theatre, Exeter. Designed by William Holford and Partners, and the author

The professional is not so well placed in England. There is small choice of *form* of playhouse in which to experiment. America is more richly provided – many foundations have endowed experimental and flexible playhouses; Greek and Elizabethan theatres have been recreated. In Canada the theatre at Stratford, Ontario has proved an inspiration to many directors, designers and actors – the first of the new open stages. The theatre at Chichester in England was to follow roughly the same pattern. The workshop theatre at LAMDA in London with its small scale was able to be more flexible and provide proscenium, open and arena staging – as does the larger and more ambitious Northcote Devon Theatre at Exeter (see fig 28).

THE FUTURE

More playhouses are being planned and built – some in open stage form, some arena, some flexible. Not many are being built with the conventional proscenium shape, because at last the local authorities, the universities, the amateurs and the architects are catching on to what has been proclaimed for close on sixty years – that our theatres are incapable of adaptation to the many kinds of drama available and also to experiment; they are, in fact, out of date.

In London, the long struggle for a National Theatre, started by Granville-Barker and William Archer in 1904, has at last been resolved, and building should have begun by the time these words are in print. Everywhere there is the same tremendous upsurge of interest in the theatre.

How can the designer contribute? Not by building mountains of naturalistic scenery that the films can do so much better, but by looking at things through a burning glass; by distilling the essence of a play; by selection of the significant detail, and rejection of the unimportant comment; by anger and compassion, by excitement and discipline; by looking and listening; and by trying to understand the world in which we live now.

Bibliography

BACKGROUND

The Attic Theatre by A. E. Haigh
Oxford University Press, London 1898

Greek Tragedy by H. D. F. Kitto
Methuen and Co. Ltd, London 1939

The Art of Greek Comedy by K. Lever
Methuen and Co. Ltd, London 1956

The Roman Stage by W. Beare
Methuen and Co. Ltd, London 1950

The Natyasastra by Bharata, translated Gosh
Royal Asiatic Society, London 1950

The Classical Drama of India by H. W. Wells
Asia Publishing House, London 1963

The Classical Theatre of China by A. C. Scott
Allen and Unwin Ltd, London 1957

Chinese Theatre by Kolvodova, Sis and Vanis, translated Iris Urwin
Springbooks, London 1959

The No Plays of Japan by Arthur Waley
Allen and Unwin Ltd, London 1921

The Kabuki Theatre of Japan by A. C. Scott
Allen and Unwin Ltd, London 1955

Kabuki by Hamamura, Sugawara, Kinoshita and Minami
Tokyo 1956

MIDDLE DISTANCE AND FOREGROUND

The Medieval Stage by Sir E. K. Chambers
Oxford University Press, London 1903

The Elizabethan Stage by Sir E. K. Chambers
Oxford University Press, London 1923

The Irresistible Theatre, Vol I by W. Bridges Adams
Secker and Warburg Ltd, London 1957

The Globe Restored by C. Walter Hodges
Ernest Benn Ltd, London 1953

The Renaissance Stage, edited by B. Hewitt
University of Miami 1958

Designs by Inigo Jones by Simpson and Bell
Malone Society, 1924

Stuart Masques by Allardyce Nicoll
George G. Harrap and Co. Ltd, London 1937

Restoration Comedy by Bonamy Dobrée
Oxford University Press, London 1924

Restoration Tragedy by Bonamy Dobrée
Oxford University Press, London 1929

The Magnificence of Eszterhaza by Matyas Horanyi
Barrie and Rockliff Ltd, London 1962

Early Victorian Drama by Ernest Reynolds
W. Heffer and Sons Ltd, Cambridge 1936

The Last Actor Managers by Hesketh Pearson
Methuen and Co. Ltd, London 1950

The New Soviet Theatre by Joseph Macleod
Allen and Unwin Ltd, London 1943

Theatre in Soviet Russia by Andre Van Gyseghem
Faber and Faber Ltd, London 1943

The Theatre of the Absurd by Martin Esslin
Eyre and Spottiswoode Ltd, London 1962

Brecht on Theatre, translated by J. Willet
Methuen and Co. Ltd, London 1964

GENERAL

English Dramatic Literature by A. G. Ward
Macmillan and Co. Ltd, London 1875

The Art of the Theatre by E. G. Craig
G. T. Foulis and Co. Ltd, London 1905

On the Art of the Theatre by E. G. Craig
Heinemann Ltd, London 1911

The Theatre by Sheldon Cheyney
Tudor Publishing Company, New York 1929

The Stage is Set by Lee Simonson
Dover Publications Inc., New York 1932

New Theatres for Old by Mordekai Gorelik
Dobson Books Ltd, London 1940

The Oxford Companion to the Theatre, edited by Phyllis Hartnoll
Oxford University Press, London 1951

The Development of the Theatre by Allardyce Nicoll
George G. Harrap and Co. Ltd, London 1956

The Seven Ages of Theatre by Richard Southern
Faber and Faber Ltd, London 1962

ILLUSTRATIONS OF SCENIC DESIGN

Design in the Theatre by G. Sherringham and J. Laver
Studio Books, London 1927

The New Movement in the Theatre by L. Moussinac
B. T. Batsford Ltd, London 1931

Settings and Costumes by T. Komisarjevsky
Studio Books, London 1933

Theatre in Action by G. Whitworth
Studio Books, London 1938

The Art of Scenic Design by Lee Simonson
Harper and Rowe, New York 1950

Stage Design Throughout the World Since 1935, edited by R. Hainaux
George G. Harrap and Co. Ltd, London 1956

Stage Design Throughout the World Since 1950, edited by R. Hainaux
George G. Harrap and Co. Ltd, London 1964

PRACTICAL BOOKS

Stage Setting by R. Southern
Faber and Faber Ltd, London 1937

Proscenium and Sight Lines by R. Southern
Faber and Faber Ltd, London 1939

Designing and Painting Scenery by H. Melvill
Barrie and Rockliff Ltd, London 1948

Stage Lighting by F. Bentham
Sir Isaac Pitman and Sons Ltd, London 1950

Changeable Scenery by R. Southern
Faber and Faber Ltd, London 1952

An International Vocabulary of Technical Theatre Terms in Eight Languages, edited by R. Southern and K. Rae
Max Reinhardt Ltd, London 1959

Scene Painting and Design by S. Joseph
Sir Isaac Pitman and Sons Ltd, London 1964

A Method of Lighting the Stage by S. McCandless
Theatre Art Books, New York

Glossary of Terms

Where usage differs, the English word is followed by its American equivalent in italics.

APRON part of the stage which projects beyond the proscenium line into the auditorium

ARENA acting area totally or partly surrounded by audience

BACKCLOTH *backdrop*

BACKING flat or cloth to complete scene outside a door or window

BARREL or BAR *pipe*. Iron tube suspended horizontally above the stage by counterweights for hanging scenery or lighting

BATTEN length of timber to which cloths are attached at the top and bottom for rolling or hanging. Short lengths of batten, usually 3 × 1 in., are used for reinforcing and repairing rostrums, and for extra rails on flats to support pictures, etc.

BATTEN (electrical) see compartment batten below

BOOK FLAT *two fold flat*

BOOMERANG or BOOM vertical arrangement of spotlights in wings

BORDER horizontal flat or shallow curtain, hung above the stage to conceal lighting and scenery suspended from grid

BOX SET setting enclosing the stage with a run of flats representing the walls of a room

BRACE support for a flat

BRAIL LINE *guide line*. Rope or sash line for adjusting position of hanging scenery

CARPET CUT long narrow trap at front of stage, used to secure front of carpet or stage cloth

CENTRE LINE line bisecting the stage from front to back, shown on the ground plan and chalked on the stage when setting up

CLEAT attachment on back of flat for securing a throwline. Also affixed to fly rail for tying off hemp lines

CLOTH *drop*

COMPARTMENT BATTEN *border light*. Trough of small, boxed floodlights wired in three or four independent circuits in front of which colour mediums can be slid. Used above the stage for general light, on stage floor to light a cloth or cyclorama, and in front of the stage as footlights

COUNTERWEIGHT SYSTEM mechanical method of balancing the weight of scenery to be hung from the grid

CRADLE housing for counterweights

CUT slit in stage floor by which means wings were run on and off in the old days. Now any long narrow trap running across stage

CUT CLOTH *cutout drop*

CUTOUT Plywood covered flat with shapes cut out, or canvas covered with gauze reinforcement

CYCLORAMA curved backcloth usually painted in one colour, partly encompassing the acting area and indicating sky

DIMMER general term for various appliances – transformers, rheostats, etc., by which the quantity of light can be graded

DIP *floor pocket*. Small metal trap in stage floor, covering sockets into which leads for floods, ground row lights, backing strips, fires, etc., can be plugged

DOCK scene store at the side or back of stage with direct access to street for loading

DOWNSTAGE nearest the audience

EXTENDING BRACE *extension brace*. Adjustable support for a flat

FALSE PROSCENIUM *portal opening*. Temporary proscenium set within the permanent opening

FESTOON curtain with several lines passing through rings sewn to webbing on the reverse side. By this means the curtain can be draped in swags

FLAT wooden frame covered with canvas, usually representing a wall

FLOATS footlights

FLOOD lamp with a diffusing reflector giving a wide spread of light; suspended above stage or used on a stand in wings

FLY FLOOR narrow gallery above stage (usually on both side walls) from which suspended scenery and lighting can be raised and lowered. Sometimes fly bridge across back wall connects fly floors on each side

FLY RAIL *pinrail*. Railing on stage side of fly floor to which hemp lines are made off on a cleat

FOOTLIGHTS diffused lighting in front of stage at floor level usually in compartments

FORESTAGE another word for apron

FRENCH BRACE *jack.* Wooden support hinged to a flat

FRENCH FLAT two or three flats battened together for flying

FRONT OF HOUSE (F.O.H.) LIGHTING *auditorium beam.* Spotlights in the auditorium focused on the front of the stage

FROST a gelatin resembling frosted or ground glass for diffusing light

GAUZE fine woven mesh that can be painted or dyed to look solid when lit from in front, transparent when front light removed and stage lit behind

GELATIN colour medium for lighting

GET IN *take in*

GET OUT *take out*

GRID steel framework above the stage from which scenery and lighting is suspended

GROUND ROW flat on its side, often with profiled edge, painted to represent middle or far distance. Functionally it conceals lighting of backcloth, cyclorama, etc.

GROOVE old-fashioned method of sliding on and off backscenes or wing flats

GRUMMET *grommet.* Line of rope or wire with release snap hook

HANGING IRON iron plate with ring, screwed to flat for flying

HEMP LINE man-handled line, as opposed to counterweighted line

HOUSE CURTAIN permanent front curtain (tabs)

LEG *leg drop.* Masking between wings and borders, running up and down stage

LIFT *elevator*

LINE rope suspended from grid. In average sized theatre there are three – short, centre and long

LOADING FLOOR *loading bridge.* Gallery above fly floor from which cradles are loaded

MASK to seal gaps in setting by adjusting backings, borders, wings and legs, etc., from the viewpoint of the most extreme sightlines

OPPOSITE PROMPT (O.P.) *stage right*

PACK *stack.* Scenery in wings or dock ready for use

PAGEANT *parabolic reflector flood.* Strong directional light, slightly diffused. Now more or less replaced by soft edge spot

PAINT FRAME large vertical frame on to which a cloth or a run of flats is nailed for painting from a bridge. The frame or bridge can be raised or lowered

PERCH *tormentor spot.* Downstage spotlight behind the side of the proscenium, usually above head height

PIANO WIRE virtually invisible from the front, used for flying when grummet impractical, and hemp line would show. Often painted to match background, or wound with black insulating tape

PLATE *keystone.* Plywood piece for reinforcing a joint on any kind of frame, particularly used with a butt joint

PRIMING preparatory coat of size and paint on new canvas, or obliterating coat on old canvas to be repainted

PROFILE FLAT flat with plywood edge cut in silhouette

PROFILE SPOT hard edge spotlight

PROJECTOR spotlight designed to throw a painted or photographic slide on to a backcloth or screen. Also to throw a silhouette across stage or on the floor (window bars, shadows of leaves, etc.)

PROMPT SIDE (P.S.) *stage left*

PROPERTIES (PROPS) pieces used in the action of the play too small to qualify as scenery. The word originated at Drury Lane when Garrick had 'Property of the Management' painted or sewn on any movable object

PROSCENIUM originally Latin version of Greek word meaning 'in front of the tent' (dressing room). Now means the frame dividing conventional auditorium from stage

RAIL horizontal member of flat frame

RAKE slope, either of whole stage or of ramped rostrum

RETURN flat leading 'off' at right angle to another

REVEAL *thickness.* Surround of arch, window, door, etc., at right angle to face of flat

ROSTRUM *parallel.* Platform for raising a part of the stage

SANDWICH BATTEN double battening for cloths

SETTING LINE line parallel with footlights, upstage of house curtain from which setting of scenery is measured. Must be shown on designer's ground plan

SILL *saddle iron.* Flat iron bar spanning the foot of a door opening or archway for strength

SIZE *sizing.* Thin glue in powder or gelatin form which acts as a fixative to scene paint

SPOT BAR *light pipe.* Counterweighted barrel from which spotlights are hung above stage

SPOT LINE single line dropped from the grid to an exact mark on the stage

STAGE CLOTH *ground cloth*

STAGE DIRECTOR *production stage manager*

STAGE SCREW screw for securing stage brace to floor

STAGE WEIGHT weight for holding stage brace in position

STILE vertical member of flat frame

SWAG curtain with a line passing through rings sewn on reverse (most effectively in a curve) to achieve a diagonal drape. A weight is needed on the bottom ring to lower the swag

TABS tableaux curtains. Usually applied to house curtain, but can be hung anywhere

THROWLINE *lashline*. Line temporarily securing two flats together by means of cleats and a slip knot

TOGGLE *keystone*. Means of attaching centre rail(s) of the frame of a flat to the stiles. These rails are hence known as toggle rails

TORMENTOR masking flat immediately behind the proscenium running upstage as far as the setting line and/or false proscenium

TRANSPARENCY cloth or part of a cloth of linen, painted in dye colours to be lit from behind

TRAP trapdoor cut anywhere in stage floor between joists

TRAVERSE CURTAIN *traveler*

TRUCK *waggon*. Rostrum on wheels, carrying a setting or part of a setting

WINGS sides of stage not in view of audience; so called after wing flats set each side of acting area parallel to setting line or angled upstage, painted as part of scene or for formal masking

Index *numbers in italics refer to plate numbers*